7 INSIGHTS INTO SAFETY LEADERSHIP

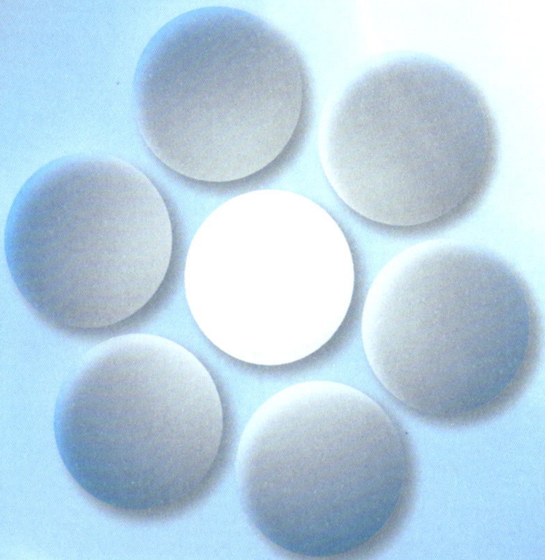

Thomas R. Krause and Kristen J. Bell

7 Insights into Safety Leadership
by Thomas R. Krause and Kristen J. Bell

Printed in the United States of America
First Edition. Fourteenth Printing.

Published by The Safety Leadership Institute
Editing by Kendra Greene
Book Design by Erica Mena
Cover Design and Illustrations by Andy Gilman

Library of Congress Cataloging-in-Publication Data
7 Insights into Safety Leadership
by Thomas R. Krause and Kristen J. Bell — 1st ed.
p. cm.
ISBN 978-0-9966859-0-0 (pbk.)
1. Industrial Safety. 2. Safety Leadership
I. Krause, Thomas R., 1944 —. II. Bell, Kristen J., 1968—.
Library of Congress Control Number: 2015913881

The Safety Leadership Institute

CONTENTS

ACKNOWLEDGMENTS

The authors wish to acknowledge our clients and colleagues whose collective work and experience with us yielded the *7 Insights* set forth in this book.

This book represents the culmination of a collective 60 years' experience in organizational safety leadership, experience that is defined by every interaction with our clients, colleagues, employees, and especially our toughest critics. We are grateful to those thousands of leaders, managers, and safety professionals whom we have met who insist on bringing the best information, experience, technology and ideas forward in order to improve safety and to prevent serious injuries and fatalities: leaders who had the vision to innovate with us and the commitment to learning in the process.

We are especially grateful to Kathy Gerwig, whose invitation to Dr. Krause to present his "Insights into Safety Excellence" talk to her colleagues at Kaiser Permanente planted the seed to write this book. Kathy, along with many other individuals, influenced us and shaped our thinking on this topic. They include: Lindsay Booher at ExxonMobil; Michael Coplen at the Federal Railroad Administration; Michael Damasin of Cargill; Lucie Dionne, when she was at Petro-Canada; Jeff Hedges of Chevron Corporation; Jim Howe when he was at the United Auto Workers Health and Safety Department, currently at Safety Solutions; Glenn Murray of ExxonMobil; Steve Newell of ORCHSE; Sean O'Keefe, when he was at NASA; Paul O'Neill, when he was at International Paper, Alcoa, the US Treasury, and now The Blackstone Group; Tom Raslear, when he was at the Federal Railroad Administration and now at the Institutes for Behavior Resources; James Robinson, when he was at Hess Corporation, now at Oil Search Ltd.; and Jeffrey Shockey at Alcoa.

We thank our colleagues at BST who we 'grew up with' and who inspired us to be better: Don Groover, John Hidley, Gennifer Lyon, Jim Spigener, Larry Russell, Scott Stricoff, Rebecca Timmons, Tom Weekley and the incredible bench of consultants and staff that deliver BST projects.

We thank all those who collaborated with us on the writing, editing, and publication of this book. Kendra Greene edited our writing. Erica Mena contributed the layout. Andrew Gilman designed the graphics, and Jessica Adams pulled everything together.

Finally, we wish to thank our families for their support and encouragement, and for being the biggest reason we do what we do.

FOREWORD

During more than 40 years in the safety and health profession, I have heard business leaders give the "safety is important" speech on many occasions. Each time I appreciate those remarks because I believe they reflect a heartfelt commitment to the safety and health mission.

Most business leaders want to operate high-performance workplaces that ensure effective worker protection. The problem is that they often don't know how to get there. And when they ask safety and health professionals for guidance, we often don't know what to tell them to do.

That is why *7 Insights into Safety Leadership* is a 'must-read' for those committed to promoting safety excellence. Although much has been written on the topic of safety leadership, new information, especially information based on hard data, is scarce. Tom Krause and Kristen Bell have taken a fresh look at safety leadership and drawn some compelling conclusions. Based on analysis of a longitudinal study that included thousands of observations, their findings not only reinforce the importance of safety leadership to the overall operation of a business, they also provide important guide posts for leaders to follow. This work builds on an earlier book that Tom wrote, *Leading With Safety,* which by itself made an important contribution to our professional knowledge base.

Why is effective safety leadership so important? Although many in industry have achieved OSHA compliance, protecting workers represents an evolving challenge. To be effective, safety and health efforts must keep pace with constantly changing work environments and increasingly complex work processes. They also must adapt to business developments such as the growing use of contract and contingent workers and the complications associated with using global supply chains.

Success in this context demands a broader view of the safety function than has been traditionally embraced by some. Maintaining staff with technical expertise in safety is important, but not sufficient, to meet the potential threats posed by these dynamic forces. Safety must be part of the fabric of the organization, embraced by everyone from workers on the shop floor to executives in the C-Suite.

This is where safety leadership comes in. Aside from controlling resources, business leaders set the tone and the expectations for the enterprise. They are uniquely positioned to make a huge contribution to the safety and health mission. In the alternative, if they inadvertently send the wrong signals they can foster some of the worst damage. That is why most of us recognize that leadership commitment and support is a key element of an effective safety and health management system. When it comes to worker safety and health, business leaders need to ***get it right***.

There is another reason why I believe that this book is important – something that has special meaning for me personally. For the past decade I have been immersed in an effort to develop better methods for fatality and serious injury prevention.

We are on the threshold of a renaissance in safety and health thinking. The change is being driven by the growing realization that techniques that have worked well over the years to reduce overall OSHA injury and illness rates have not had a similar impact on the injuries and illnesses that cause the greatest loss and human suffering. Fatalities, life-threatening events, and severe injuries and illnesses that are life altering, continue at unacceptable levels. The ongoing loss is attributed to the insufficiency of current approaches and to several concepts that have underpinned our profession for decades but which may actually be barriers to serious injury and illness prevention.

One of the key contributors to the emerging body of thought on this topic has been Tom Krause, who, while at BST, led a ground-breaking task force (described later in this book) that identified key factors contributing to serious incidents. My company and several of our members were fortunate to have participated in some of that earlier work with Tom.

Prevention efforts historically have been centered on the interaction between the hazard, the controls, and the employee who has been injured or made ill. Emphasis has been on compliance and on holding workers accountable for their actions. Corrective actions have traditionally focused on 'fixing' the injured/ill employee who 'messed up,' largely through retraining or by applying more administrative controls. Insufficient attention has been paid to the role the organization played in contributing to the event.

Deficiencies in that approach have led to a growing belief that a new paradigm for preventing serious incidents is needed. Consequently, we launched an initiative earlier this year under our own banner, ORCHSE Strategies, LLC. We are a membership-based consulting firm with safety, health, and environmental networks that include 120 large global corporations in 20 different industrial sectors. A small group of experts from industry, labor, aviation, nuclear power, and other relevant disciplines was convened to provide greater clarity around key factors that contribute to catastrophic events and, if needed, to begin fleshing out a new approach to prevention. A new view of safety and health seems to be emerging from that work and from the work of other dedicated and knowledgeable safety and health professionals.

This new approach provides a context in which to view the important lessons learned... lessons that are shared in this book.

And the authors' findings provide valuable insights that impact and enhance the new view.

The emerging body of thought suggests that a broader view of the forces that drive serious incidents is needed. This requires a richer understanding of how work actually gets done, consideration of the context in which employees must cope with hazards, and assessment of an organization's capacity to deal with risks that have high severity potential. Human factors are identified and addressed along with organizational attributes (e.g., cultural characteristics, management system gaps, process conditions) that can undermine defenses and elevate risk. Corrective actions focus more on fixing the system than on fixing the employee.

This book has relevance for that effort because ***effective safety leadership*** is critical to creating a learning organization that has the intellect, capacity, and guts to identify and rectify systems issues within the organization. Simply put, *our efforts to enhance serious injury prevention will not succeed without it.*

The findings in *7 Insights into Safety Leadership* will benefit both safety professionals and the leaders that we are trying to influence. Protecting workers requires effectively identifying, prioritizing, and managing a wide range of risks; and while large companies frequently employ EH&S experts and risk managers, CEOs and senior business leaders ultimately bear the burden – and experience the sleepless nights – when there is uncertainty or, worse yet, tragedy.

In short, safety leadership is more important than ever. I congratulate Tom and Kristen on this effort and implore them to continue to build on this important work.

Stephen A. Newell
Partner,
ORCHSE Strategies, LLC.

INTRODUCTION

About 20 years ago, a group of us working at the safety consulting firm, BST, came together to quantify our clients' safety improvements and examine their results over a long period of time. We invited every organization we were working with to participate in a longitudinal study. About one third of them, 73 organizations representing a wide variety of industries, followed through and each of those provided four years of per-intervention data, as well as a set of follow-up data complete up to the time of the study. We calculated their improvement each year after their interventions started. Across the 73 organizations, the average improvement in injury frequency over the first year was 26% and it continued to increase, reaching 69% improvement in the fifth year. This was clear and compelling evidence that our methods (see Chapter 6) were effective across a wide range of organizations, and we published the findings in a peer-reviewed journal, *Safety Science*.[i]

Although we were pleased with the rigor of the study and its contribution to the field, those results were not all that interesting to us: They were expected. Far more interesting was the finding we did not expect: We found more variation across the 73 organizations than we anticipated, and we saw different patterns of variation than we had anticipated. When we examined the results of each individual organization, many achieved more than 50% improvement in the first year and continued to improve year after year. Some organizations stayed level for a while, and then improved. A handful of organizations *increased* their injury rates initially and improved later on. One organization got worse in the first year, worse still in the second, and never saw improvement over the course of the study. So while the average improvement was significant, we wanted to understand the variation. We decided to dig deeper. We decided to find out what distinguished the very successful organizations from the rest of the pack.

The answers came from a series of studies designed to isolate the factors most likely responsible for the success or failure of organization-wide safety improvement initiatives. At the center of this body of work was an "extreme-groups" study in which we selected organizations that had achieved extraordinary improvement.[ii] For these organizations, we were able to find a similar organization that had achieved below-average improvement. The pairs of organizations represented the same industries, the same labor unions, and had similar baseline incident rates, sizes, and even start dates. In other words, we had pairs of sites doing similar work with similar people under similar circumstances, both sites using the same safety improvement methodology, yet they were experiencing dramatically different results. We sent a team of people to each location where they interviewed people, observed them in action, and audited their safety improvement efforts. We discovered that the primary differentiating factor was the strength of the safety leadership. Every other study in the series replicated and supported the central role of leadership in the success of safety improvement initiatives. Much of this work was summarized in our book, *Leading with Safety.*[iii]

Such a finding might seem obvious today, now that the importance of organizational safety leadership is broadly acknowledged, but we did not expect to discover this 20 years ago when we were working with teams of front-line employees to implement a safety improvement system with minimal direct involvement from management. The roles of managers and supervisors were narrowly defined to support our intervention: We were not looking at the role of managers in safety generally.

Discovering the relationship between leadership and safety improvement was a breakthrough, and the beginning of an understanding that continues to evolve. Today, there is a strong body of research on leadership behaviors important to safety. We understand the mechanisms that connect leader behavior to performance. Despite this progress, we still find one aspect of safety leadership that remains elusive among leadership: It's that gut-level sense that somebody really 'Gets' why safety matters on a human level and how to use those values to make a safer workplace.

We have met countless safety professionals and dozens of executives who 'Get It.' We think of Jim Dietz at PotashCorp, or Glenn Murray at ExxonMobil, and the thousands of others we have had the privilege of working with over the years. The safety professionals we know who 'Get It' have devoted their careers to protecting others. These are professionals who witnessed the pain and suffering resulting from fatalities and life-altering injuries, and responded both by deepening their care and compassion and by strengthening their resolve to prevent future tragedy. Their personal experiences gave them inimitable motivation, and it has been their professional background, training, and understanding of organizational dynamics that's given them the know-how to make an impact.

Unfortunately, too many gifted safety professionals are limited by their lack of formal authority within the organizations they serve. In many organizations, the top safety professional does not have a seat at the executive table. The top safety professional does not even always report directly to the CEO. In these organizations, the safety function is subordinate to other functions in the business, which dilutes its power and limits its influence—*unless* the leaders in positions of greater authority are also individuals who 'Get It,' especially the CEO.

If you doubt the roles that organizational structure and power play in safety, consider NASA's experience. When NASA was created in 1958, it did not have a formal, identifiable safety function on its organizational chart. After the Apollo 1 disaster in 1967, NASA created a separate safety function, but it was not independent; its funding was linked with the very programs it was supposed to oversee. The Rogers Commission investigating the Challenger accident of 1986 cited the lack of independent safety oversight at NASA as a *basic deficiency* in NASA's safety system. And in 2003, the Columbia Accident Investigation Board said NASA's safety program "*is flawed by its dependence on the Shuttle Program … An independent safety structure would provide the Shuttle Program a more effective operational safety process.*"[iv]

Whether the formal organizational structure reflects it or not, the senior-most executive *is* the senior-most safety leader in the business. Rex Tillerson, Chairman and CEO of ExxonMobil acknowledged this to international business leaders when he said, "Fundamentally, this is what we do. We are in the risk management business."[v] Whatever it is your company produces, and whatever your job title says, you are first and foremost in the safety business.

Unfortunately, relatively few senior leaders really, truly 'Get Safety.' We have been fortunate to personally work with some who do: People like Sean O'Keefe at NASA and Paul O'Neill at Alcoa, who not only have the personal drive to protect human life, but who also understand which levers to pull and why. Compared to safety professionals whose professional identities center on their roles as safety leaders, far fewer senior leaders in organizations have personally invested themselves in safety. We've found that unless a person has learned from direct personal experience with life-threatening, life-altering, or life-ending events, they are unlikely to take on safety as their personal calling. Even among executives who have a strong motivation to lead safety for their organizations, many do not understand what they need to do in order to achieve their goals: They need a different understanding of safety than most business leaders have today. That's what motivated us to write this book.

CRITICAL INSIGHTS THAT EFFECTIVE SAFETY LEADERS NEED TO HAVE

So what is it that senior leaders need to 'Get' about safety? What is it that these key safety leaders need in order to influence the organization and achieve better and better performance? We've devoted more than 20 years to figuring this out, and our research has yielded seven critical insights. This book is all about the acumen that every leader must understand and employ in order to reach safety leadership excellence.

1. SAFETY PERFORMANCE LEADS BUSINESS PERFORMANCE

The first insight is about the relationship between safety and organizational performance. When a senior leader understands how safety and organizational performance are connected and why they are connected, it will affect the way they think about their strategy and vision for the organization.

2. SAFETY LEADERSHIP STARTS WITH ATTENTION TO SERIOUS INJURIES AND FATALITIES

The second insight into safety excellence is that senior leaders should focus attention first on addressing serious injuries and fatalities (SIFs). The long-held practice of concentrating on minor incidents and hoping for a trickle up effect has been proven inadequate, and leadership needs to familiarize itself with the most serious risks.

3. LEADERSHIP SETS SAFETY IMPROVEMENT IN MOTION

The third insight has to do with how safety leadership sets the stage for safety improvement, and why safety leadership is the starting point for successful organizational change. It answers the question, "What does it mean to 'Get It' when it comes to leading safety, and where does 'It' come from?"

4. CULTURE SUSTAINS PERFORMANCE—FOR BETTER OR FOR WORSE

Leadership affects culture, and culture amplifies everything. The fourth insight is about the role culture plays in safety and organizational performance generally. It explains the very interesting relationships between leadership and culture, and implications for the long-term future of the organization.

5. SAFE DECISION MAKING IS BUILT ON THE UNDERSTANDING OF CORE SAFETY CONCEPTS

The fifth insight has to do with injury causation and prevention. It offers core concepts about injury causation that inform and guide strategies for decision making and safety improvement.

6. UNDERSTANDING THE ROLE OF BEHAVIOR IN SAFETY PERFORMANCE IMPROVEMENT

The sixth insight is about the role of behavior in organizational safety. It tracks the history of Behavior-Based Safety (BBS) efforts and explains why BBS is controversial and poorly understood. It shows how the term "BBS" has been abused as well as how it was originally defined and successfully implemented.

7. COGNITIVE BIAS AFFECTS SAFETY DECISIONS

The seventh insight has to do with safe decision making and some of the ways cognitive bias undermines our judgment. It discusses several biases that affect decisions we make in leading and managing safety—as well as individual risk-taking decisions—and how those biases can misdirect efforts to improve.

With the benefit of hindsight, it's easy to see why our 1999 study showed the effects that it did: The 73 organizations improved their safety performance because they created safer workplaces. They analyzed data to understand where there were opportunities to improve the safety of the workplace. In the process, we saw individuals at every level becoming more effective safety leaders, which in turn improved the culture around safety.[1] People who had never understood how to improve safety began using data and technology to make better safety decisions. And while we did not set out to improve business performance explicitly, we were not surprised when organizations reported being more efficient, effective, and productive as their safety improvement strategies took hold.

But back then, we were doing a lot of things—and our clients were doing a lot of things—in an effort to improve. When we implemented a safety improvement strategy, it was impossible to know precisely which of our many efforts were producing the impact: We had not isolated the active ingredients. We did not know in what order things needed to be set in motion, or if order even mattered. We have a lot more data now, and a lot more clarity.

The seven insights presented in this book teach organizational leaders how to become excellent in safety on purpose. In a world where work is inherently risky and exposure to risk is ever-changing, organizations must be clear on their value for safety and the data-driven approaches that will chart their progress. The insights in this book are drawn from decades of research and the latest thinking. They will help leaders understand why good intentions are only the start for a safer workplace, how to sidestep common misinterpretations that can derail safety efforts, and why leaders at every level need to engage with safety—with a focus on preventing the most serious events first. Every person and

1. Here, we use the term 'culture' in a colloquial sense. We're talking about the way people think and speak and act with regard to safety.

every organization has the opportunity to be excellent at safety. It is good for your people, it is good for your culture, and excellence in safety will show up as excellence in other areas of performance. You can be more efficient and effective in your organization. You can be insightful. Safety is not such an enigma when you get this stuff.

REFERENCES

i Krause, T. R., Seymour (Bell), K. J., & Sloat, K. C. M. (1999). Long-term evaluation of a behavior-based method for improving safety performance: A meta-analysis of 73 interrupted time-series replications. *Safety Science, 32*, 1-18.

ii Hidley, J. H. (1998). Critical success factors for behavior-based safety. *Professional Safety*, 30-34.

iii Krause, T.R. (2005). *Leading with safety.* Hoboken, NJ: Wiley.

iv CAIB (Columbia Accident Investigation Board). 2003. Report, Volume 1. Government Printing Office, Washington, DC. http://www.nasa.gov/columbia/home/CAIB_Vol1.html

v Tillerson, R. W. (2007). International Business Leaders Program Address. Speech presented at Chatham House, Thursday June 21, 2007. London, England.

CHAPTER 1

SAFETY PERFORMANCE LEADS BUSINESS PERFORMANCE

If a client came to us saying, "We know we have some leadership and culture issues: Upward communication is poor, skill level of supervisors and managers in inconsistent, our people don't understand system thinking, and behavioral reliability is sketchy. We want to develop a high performance culture. How should we approach it?" Our answer would likely be, "Why not start with safety?" It is a worthwhile issue in itself: safety saves lives and lowers costs. Plus, the indirect effects are also powerful: To the extent that you develop real excellence in safety, you will also create a high performance culture—which will improve your effectiveness and efficiency in general.

Over the years, we have observed that organizations that are great at safety tend to be good at everything they do. That might seem obvious today, but it hasn't always been. Remember that when OSHA began monitoring and holding U.S. organizations accountable for their safety performance in 1970, the new legislation was seen as a burden. Safety programs were initially treated as a cost of doing business and measured in terms of lower insurance claims and reduced workers' compensation premiums, but all of that is different today. Today, the best safety programs are evaluated in terms of their impact on organizational performance.

A key shift in focus came when we discovered the relationships between safety performance, leadership, culture, and organizational performance generally. Organizations have saved millions of dollars by improving safety performance alone, but what they value above those savings is how safety engagement transforms their cultures. Trust increases, engagement is more consistent, and leadership improves. The first insight into safety excellence is that *safety performance leads business performance.*

SAFETY BRINGS PEOPLE TOGETHER

When we talk about safety, we are talking about safety in every sense, including personal safety, process safety, product safety, patient safety, security, and health. Safety represents a basic human need. Nobody is against safety, and everyone has a stake.

In the early days of behavior-based safety, clients used to ask us whether union organizations had different outcomes compared to non-union organizations. The prevailing belief at the time was that adversarial relationships between managers and workers in unionized companies would dampen the benefits of a safety initiative that depended on employee engagement. Yet in a study comparing the improvement in safety performance between 77 union and 75 non-union sites, the results showed no difference.[i] To be sure, we certainly did observe strained relationships between managers and workers in some of these organizations, but safety was important enough that they found ways to work together.

Indeed, safety brings people together across all levels and functions to contribute to a common goal. Each person in an organization is responsible for safety, and every individual is uniquely positioned to identify, create, and mitigate exposure for himself and others. When people start looking out for one another's safety, it brings them together in other ways. They start talking to each other, communicating more, and identifying and resolving problems together. Dealing with common safety issues provides opportunities to interact, influence, and participate that might not otherwise occur within an organization.

SAFETY CULTIVATES LEADERSHIP

When workers and first-level supervisors get involved in safety, they often find themselves in positions where they need to influence without authority. We find that they learn to build support through social and interpersonal means instead of relying solely on political or positional authority. Social influence is a powerful skill to have, and safety provides the means and opportunities to develop this aspect of leadership.

We have worked with corporate HR departments to compare, contrast, and align their general leadership competencies with the safety leadership best practices and behaviors introduced through our work together. In every case, there has been near-perfect alignment between what they wanted generally in leadership and what we were asking for specifically in safety leadership. Where there were differences in leadership goals, we found organizations that combine managerial and technical competencies (such as planning and organizing) with leadership competencies (which are more about interpersonal influence). Yet even in these cases, safety provided ideal opportunities to cultivate and practice the desired leadership skills.

SAFETY LEADERSHIP IMPROVES ORGANIZATIONAL CULTURE, AND CULTURE ELEVATES PERFORMANCE

Safety engagement improves performance through two distinct mechanisms. One mechanism is direct: More effective efforts to identify and manage exposure lead to fewer incidents and injuries. The other mechanism is indirect: Stronger engagement and more visible leadership create a stronger organizational culture, which in turn leads to improved efficiency and effectiveness overall. The importance of this second pathway cannot be overstated: *More effective leadership and stronger culture connect excellence in safety to excellent performance generally.*

Decades of research published in peer-reviewed journals have demonstrated that the same cultural attributes that correlate with safety performance also correlate with business performance. Two such attributes have been discussed widely in this research literature: one is referred to in the studies as Perceived Organizational Support (POS) and the other as Leader-Member Exchange (LMX). POS predicts employee performance and organizational communication,[ii] organizational citizenship behavior, organizational commitment,[iii] turnover intention,[iv] job satisfaction, pay satisfaction, and strain.[v] LMX also relates to several indicators of business performance including team performance;[vi] task performance;[vii] teacher effectiveness and teacher performance;[viii] and supervisor ratings, objective job performance, and errors.[ix] When POS and LMX improve for safety, they improve throughout the organization. Relationships like these have been demonstrated for a dozen cultural attributes.[x]

LEAD WITH SAFETY

Nobody understands and champions these relationships between safety and organizational culture better than the former Secretary of the US Treasury, the honorable Paul O'Neill. The first author was privileged to meet O'Neill when he was President at International Paper Company, and continued to consult with him after he became CEO and Chairman of Alcoa in 1987. O'Neill served as CEO until 1999, and retired as chairman at the end of 2000. His tenure at Alcoa was a major success: In 1987, Alcoa's lost-time incident frequency rate was 1.86. In 2002, it was 0.12. Meanwhile, Alcoa's market value increased from $3 billion to $27.53 billion.

Safety played a central role in O'Neill's business strategy. In his very first address to Alcoa shareholders, he emphatically committed to safety as the first order of good business. Two decades of results bore him out, and in a 2009 address to healthcare CEOs, O'Neill discussed his strategy and his view of the irreducible components of leadership.[xi] He said, "First of all, I think it's necessary for a *real* leader to articulate what I call *unarguable goals and aspirations* for the institution that they lead." For O'Neill, zero injuries is one of those unarguable goals. "In a really great organization," he said, "the people in it are never injured at work." Who can argue with that?

Notice that O'Neill, a former Secretary of the Treasury, didn't lead with finance. He didn't set the goal of increasing market value by 900% over the next 14 years, although that is exactly what he did. As he told the healthcare CEOs, "In a truly great organization, finance is not an objective, it is a consequence. It is a consequence of being greater at what you do than anyone else." O'Neill knew that if he could get the safety part right, he could use that to build performance excellence across the organization. As Alcoa became a world leader in safety, they were increasing their capacity for growth and prosperity.

In sum, the relationships between safety, engagement, leadership, culture, and performance make safety an ideal catalyst for improving every area of a business. When safety improves significantly as the result of getting employees engaged, that not only makes the numbers better, but it also strengthens culture. And a strong culture makes it possible to achieve performance excellence in all areas of business.

If you are a leader and you have the insight described in this chapter, it will transform your relationship to safety. You will start to see opportunities to improve rather than problems to address. Your role as a decision-making leader will change. Your thinking will change, and the decisions you make will change. You will be willing to give time and energy and attention to safety. Not because someone told you to, not because it is a big thing in your company and you will be rewarded for it, but because it is something you think is important. You recognize that it matters that you do this. And that is pivotal.

REFERENCES

i. BST, Inc. (2006). *Downloads: Russell Consulting International*. Retrieved June 11, 2014, from http://www.russellconsulting.com.au/downloads/BST_Global_Capability.pdf

ii. Neves, P., & Eisenberger, R. (2012). Management communication and employee performance: The contribution of perceived organizational support. *Human Performance, 25*(5), 452-464.

iii. Currie, P., & Dollery, B. (2006). Organizational commitment and perceived organizational support in the NSW police. *Policing, 29*(4), 741-756.

iv. Dawley, D., Jeffrey, H., & Bucklew, N. (2010). Perceived organizational support and turnover intention: The mediating effects of personal sacrifice and job fit. *Journal of Social Psychology, 150*(3), 238-257.

v. Harris, R., Harris, K., & Harvey, P. (2007). A test of competing models of the relationships among perceptions of organizational politics, perceived organizational support, and individual outcomes. *Journal of Social Psychology, 147*(6), 631-656.

vi. Naidoo, L., Scherbaum, C., Goldstein, H., & Graen, G. (2011). A longitudinal examination of the effects of lmx, ability, and differentiation on team performance. *Journal of Business & Psychology, 26*(3), 347-357.

vii. Chung-Kai, L., & Chia-hung, H. (2009). The influence of transformational leadership on workplace relationships and job performance. *Social Behavior & Personality: An International Journal, 37*(8), 1129-1142.

viii. Somech, A., & Wenderow, M. (2006). The impact of participative and directive leadership on teachers' performance: the intervening effects of job structuring, decision domain, and leader-member exchange. *Educational Administration Quarterly, 42*(5), 746-772.

ix. Vecchio, R. (1998). Leader-member exchange, objective performance, employment duration, and supervisor ratings: testing for moderation and mediation. *Journal of Business & Psychology, 12*(3), 327-341.

x. Krause, T. (2005). *Leading with safety.* Hoboken, NJ: Wiley.

xi. Value Capture. (2012, March 22). *Paul O'Neill the irreducible components of leadership* [Video file]. Retrieved June 11, 2014, from http://www.youtube.com/watch?v=htLCVqaLBvo

Paul O'Neill

Paul O'Neill was the CEO of Alcoa from 1987 to 2000. Under his leadership, Alcoa's market value increased from $3 billion in 1986 to $27.53 billion in 2000, while net income increased from $200 million to $1.48 billion.

O'Neill began his first speech to Alcoa shareholders in 1987 by saying, "I want to talk to you about worker safety."

The room fell silent.

O'Neill continued, "Every year, numerous Alcoa workers are injured so badly that they miss a day of work. Our safety record is better than the general American workforce, especially considering that our employees work with metals that are 1500 degrees and machines that can rip a man's arm off. But it's not good enough. I intend to make Alcoa the safest company in America. I intend to go for zero injuries."

Charles Duhigg witnessed the silence and recounted the scene in his book, *The Power of Habit.* An investor finally asked a question; it was a question about inventories. "I'm not certain you heard me," O'Neill replied. *"If you want to understand how Alcoa is doing, you need to look at our workplace safety figures."*

Paul O'Neill understood the connection between safety and business performance, and his strategy for turning the company around centered on safety. Because of his results, today's shareholders increasingly accept the role safety can play in business success, and they want to invest in ethical, successful, competent businesses. A company's ability to manage safety reflects its ability to manage every aspect of its performance.

CHAPTER 2

SAFETY LEADERSHIP STARTS WITH ATTENTION TO SERIOUS INJURIES AND FATALITIES

About ten years ago, Krause received a call from the corporate safety director of a global organization he had been consulting with on safety leadership. The director said they had observed a disturbing pattern in their data: Recordable injuries were declining steadily over the previous five year period, but serious and fatal injuries were level during the same time period.

Senior corporate leadership had seen this information and was very concerned about it. They had discussed it for months, and the organization as a whole was perplexed. They had assumed, as most organizations have, that as their smaller injuries declined, their larger ones would as well.

They asked Krause to develop a new paradigm for the prevention of serious injuries and fatalities and bring it to a meeting of their top hundred leaders globally and present it. He took on the challenge, and over the next several months we looked at data across organizations, across industries, and across North America. We found that a similar pattern existed consistently in all areas. And the analysis changed our thinking about how we approach serious injuries and fatalities.

Put bluntly: The traditional view that preventing smaller injuries will lead to preventing larger ones has been shown to be false. The second insight into safety excellence is that *safety leadership should begin with attention to serious injuries and fatalities (SIFs).* We'll show why in this chapter, and the reasons are strategic, compassionate, and research-based.

THE TRADITIONAL SAFETY TRIANGLE AND THE NEW DATA

The concept of the Safety Triangle (Figure 1) was first presented by Herbert William Heinrich in 1931. It has been widely accepted by the safety community worldwide. It has two premises:

- Frequency and severity are inversely correlated. Any distribution of injuries will have a larger number of small injuries (represented at the bottom of the triangle), and a smaller number of more serious injuries (represented at the top of the triangle).
- Reducing injuries at the bottom of the triangle will also reduce injuries at the top of the triangle.

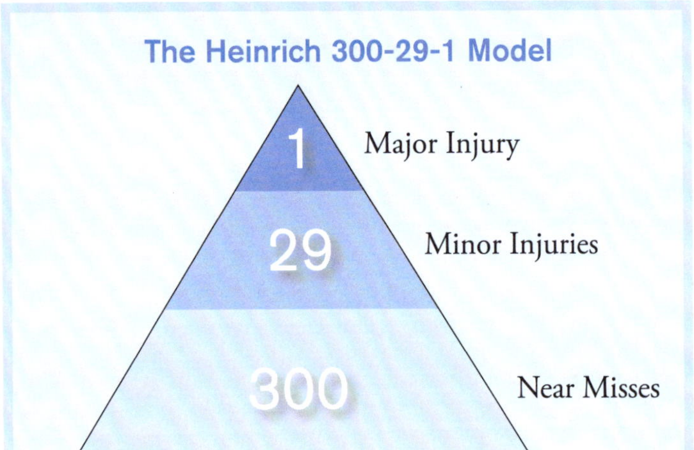

Figure 1

Yet, as we looked at that data from organizations and industries across North America, we saw a trend of non-fatal injuries steadily dropping while fatalities decreased slowly or not at all.

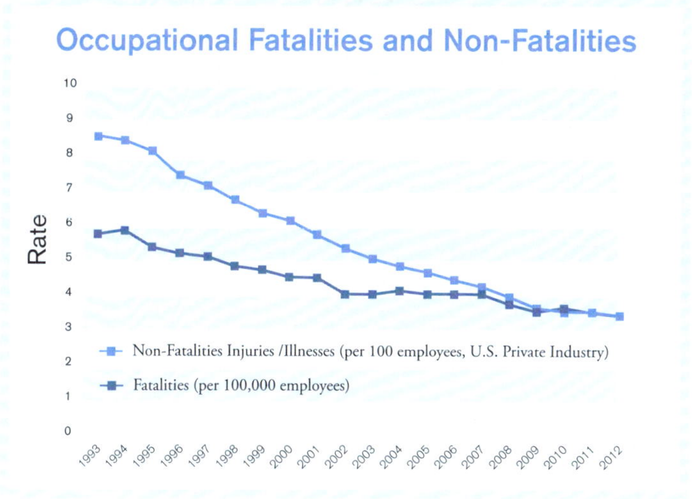

Figure 2

This pattern implicates the design and implementation of existing safety systems as inadequately addressing SIFs. It calls into question why safety systems, in general, are working to reduce smaller injuries without working specifically to address more acute events on their own terms. In short, this pattern is a very big deal, and it demands the attention of safety leaders across the organization.

Some of the safety community look at this pattern and shrug their shoulders, because it doesn't fit with a principle they've held for a long time. But unless we are willing to challenge our assumptions and understand the specific reasons for this pattern, we will not be in a position to understand what changes need to be made in order to address it. In the workplace, what this looks like at the day-to-day level is a pattern where the recordable injury frequencies of a given organization are low and either level or getting lower—and suddenly, seemingly out of the blue, a serious or fatal injury, or even a series of SIFs occur. This is a surprise to operations people, and it leaves them disappointed and perplexed.

THE STUDY

As a result of this initial data analysis, a group of global organizations came together to pool their data and study the problem. BST and ORCHSE co-sponsored the research group, which agreed with the participant organizations that the findings of the study would be held in the public domain and made available as widely as possible. The participating organizations were ExxonMobil Corporation, Archer Daniels Midland Company, BHP Billiton, PotashCorp, A.P. Moeller – Maersk Group, Cargill Inc., and Shell.

The study asked two broad questions addressing the two premises of the Safety Triangle:

1. Is the widely accepted description of the incident distribution found in the Safety Triangle accurate?

2. Are SIFs similar in nature and cause to smaller injuries?

We'll explore the findings below.

IS THE DISTRIBUTION BEHIND THE SAFETY TRIANGLE ACCURATE?

The study confirmed Heinrich's first premise; more people suffered minor injuries than major injuries, and more major injuries than serious injuries or fatalities. Figure 3 shows the combined data from all six organizations and it is clear that the distribution aspect of Heinrich's idea is correct: The inverse correlation between number of incidents and severity of incidents is an accurate and useful concept, and there was no evidence that it should be discarded.

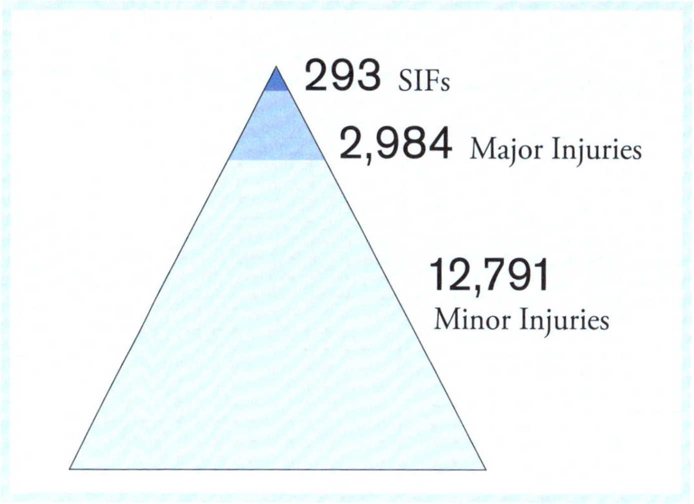

Figure 3

This finding has further implications. It also means that a single serious event is necessarily a reflection of many other events that *could have been* serious. One incident occurs every x times when the potential for an incident exists. Drunk drivers don't have accidents each time they drive. Yet, single incidents tell us about the whole system. It takes a set of variables happening at the same time to produce an incident. For instance, the driver is drunk, the car brakes are faulty, the child runs into the street when visibility is low, etc. So when an accident or incident happens, we are wrong-headed to think it is a one-time single event. The set of variables that led up to the event have happened many times previously with no incident. We know this from the Safety Triangle.

When this is not understood, misattribution manifests in reactions like the ones below:

> "This was a one-off event"

> "This catastrophic event was not related to systematic factors in the industry"

"Sometimes you step off the curb and get hit by a bus"

"We don't see a pattern in the data"

But in fact there *is* a pattern. And it points us towards a better approach to reducing SIF events.

ARE SIFS SIMILAR TO SMALLER INJURIES?

To examine whether SIFs are similar in nature and in cause to other injuries, we broke the question into two more parts:

- Do some circumstances have greater potential to lead to a serious injury or fatality than others?
- Do SIFs have different kinds of characteristics and causes than less serious injuries?

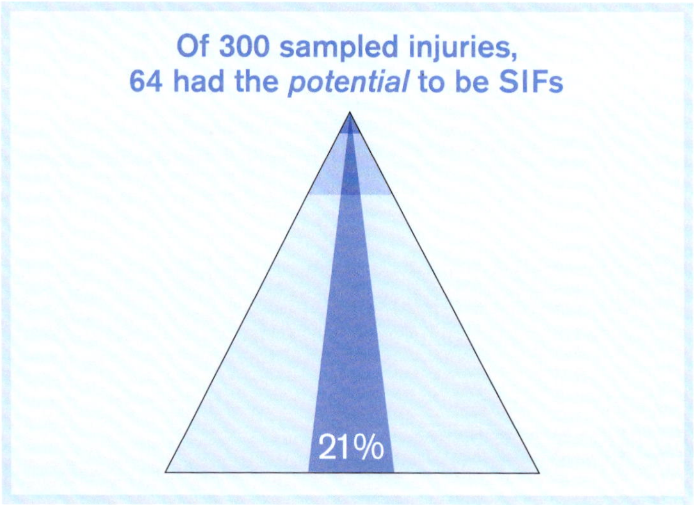

Figure 4

Figure 4 does indeed show that only a subset of smaller injuries have the potential to be serious or fatal injuries. In this sample of 300 injuries across six organizations, just 21% of smaller injuries had the potential to have been SIFs. This finding explains at least in part why some organizations see reductions of recordable injuries but not of SIFs.

This finding is a direct contradiction of the second premise of the Safety Triangle concept: *Reducing injuries at the bottom of the triangle will not necessarily reduce injuries at the top of the triangle.* This means that leaders must focus attention where it counts. Leaving it to chance and assuming that safety efforts will reach up to SIFs because they are reducing smaller injuries is a flawed strategy. *We have to start with SIFs directly.*

If leaders do not have this crucial insight they will make decisions incorrectly. For any kind of safety effort that seeks to identify hazards as a mechanism for creating a safe workplace, a leader should ask, "How do you focus attention on SIF prevention?"

SIFS HAVE DIFFERENT CHARACTERISTICS AND CAUSES

The study also found evidence that SIFs differ from minor incidents in both their characteristics and causes. For instance, it showed that Safety Absolutes (things like lock out tag out, confined space entry, fall protection) played a part in 71% of SIFs, but only 17% of less serious injuries (see Table 1 below). That's a big difference. A leader who understands this finding will target SIF prevention and ask questions like, "How do you assure that employees are able to adhere to the Safety Absolutes and do so reliably?

Table 1

	SIFs	Non-SIFs
Safety Absolutes	39 / 55 (71%)	5 / 35 (17%)

What's more, *not all injuries have SIF potential.* SIFs are disproportionately related to certain types of activities. Knowing that, identifying SIF precursors will help inform intervention strategies.

A precursor is an unmitigated high-risk situation that will result in a serious or fatal injury if allowed to continue. Here are three examples drawn from actual SIFs:

- Front-end loader operators must reposition their equipment in areas with other people working nearby. Their ability to see their paths of travel are limited by the terrain and their practice of storing extraneous material on top of the rear portion of the cabs.

- Workers repeatedly expose themselves to carbon monoxide, even after complaining of 'bad air.' They do not test the air before entering high-risk areas and they do not carry respirators.

- Pipeline inspections using poorly calibrated equipment produce erroneous measurements of metal loss due to corrosion. One pipeline that is used by three different companies is inspected and reported to be well within operating limits, when in actuality it is on the brink of failure in many places.

The leader who targets SIF prevention is concerned with the precursors of SIF events. Addressing precursors is a system-wide view that prioritizes reductions in the most severe events.

A NEW PARADIGM FOR SERIOUS INJURIES AND FATALITIES

Over the years, we have heard many variations of the following story: "I came to work the other day and found a pack of guys in ties with clipboards walking around the parking lot taking notes. It was pathetic. Do they really think they are doing something for safety? I could have shown them things in the plant that they should have been looking at."

We need a new paradigm to understand and guide prevention efforts for SIFs. The old paradigm has a valid generalization of the way incidents vary by frequency and severity, but it is misleading with respect to understanding and preventing SIFs. The old paradigm incorrectly assumed:

- All injuries of low severity have the same potential for serious injury.

- Injuries of differing severity have the same underlying causes.

- One injury reduction strategy will reach all kinds of injuries equally.

These inaccuracies of the old paradigm have been detrimental. They have resulted in elevation of trivial issues, creative classification of injuries, loss of credibility with labor organizations, cynicism among workers, and ineffective fatality prevention.

It has also been damaging to the credibility of leaders who espouse it. Think of Deepwater Horizon, where a few days before the catastrophic explosion that led to the sinking of the oil rig, 11 fatalities, and the largest oil spill in the history of the petroleum industry—the location was given a prize for excellence in safety performance.

This pattern is seen repeatedly in the analysis of SIF events. What effect does it have on the culture of the organization when leaders talk enthusiastically about the success of safety efforts, while sitting on a potential fatal event waiting to happen? Front-line employees and supervisors know of these vulnerabilities. So what they hear from leaders saying otherwise is at the very least ignorant and at worst downright hypocritical.

We can do better. What we need is a new paradigm that accounts for four key findings from the research:

- Injuries of differing severity have differing underlying causes.

- All minor injuries are not the same: A sub-set of low severity injuries are associated with precursors to serious injuries and fatalities.

- Reducing serious injuries requires a different strategy than reducing minor injuries.

- The strategy for reducing serious injuries should use precursor event data drawn from all available sources of data: accidents, injuries, near misses, and exposures.

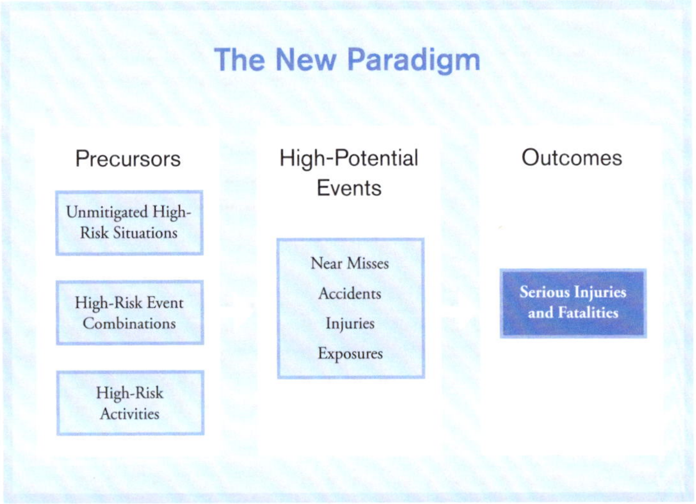

Figure 5

So keep the Safety Triangle if you want to talk about the ratios of SIFs to minor incidents; but if you want to do something to reduce SIF events, we suggest thinking in terms of the paradigm shown in Figure 5.

Focus on the potential for serious injury. Identify precursors. Precursors lead to high potential events including near misses, and high potential events lead to SIFs. The effects of the new paradigm are:

- More focused effort on the prevention of serious injuries.
- Stronger safety culture.
- More engagement of labor organizations in safety.
- Lower rates of serious injuries.

If a facility has vulnerabilities for SIFs and is not paying attention to those precursors in a systematic way, focusing on small injuries is counter-productive. It allows SIF rates to stagnate and employees to get hurt. It leaves the most senior leaders flummoxed when a serious injury occurs seemingly out of the blue—while the worker who sees the vulnerabilities day in and day out counts the event as inevitable.

Senior leaders at every level are motivated to reduce SIFs. They are frustrated by the fact that they spend time and resources on safety and still have them. That time and money is better spent—and safety professionals have better access to the tools they need to get things done—when they address SIF reduction.

Examples of Situations that May Have High Proportions of Precursor Events

Mobile equipment operation

Confined space entry

Jobs that require lock-out tag-out

Lifting operations

Working at height

Caustic liquid handling

Manual handling

Process instability

Significant process upsets

Unexpected maintenance

Unexpected changes

High energy potential jobs

Emergency shutdown procedures

CHAPTER 3

SAFETY LEADERSHIP — THE SINGLE MOST IMPORTANT THING AN ORGANIZATION CAN DO TO SET IMPROVEMENT IN MOTION

Suppose you want to accelerate the safety performance of your organization, but you have limited resources to get started. You can only invest in one of the following strategies to improve safety: You could build a stronger safety culture, improve your safety management systems, build an inherently safer facility, reduce at-risk behavior, or strengthen safety leadership.

Where would you invest your limited resources? All of these things are important, and there are merits to starting with each. For example:

- *A stronger culture* leads to all the other positive outcomes. But unless you're starting with a brand new organization, changing culture is a long-term strategy. It takes time to embed a set of shared values, beliefs, and assumptions into the fabric of an organization. And when leadership changes, the culture will also change—for better or worse.

- *Improving safety management systems* means people will have better tools for identifying and reducing risk, and it will support "systems thinking." Unfortunately, you can have the best systems in the world, and if people don't value and use them, they are worthless.

- *Building an inherently safer facility* has many advantages. It provides the opportunity to design safety into the facility. But a safe facility with a weak culture is far from optimal. If the culture is weak the facility won't be maintained properly, new decisions will overlook safety factors, and eventually conditions will degrade.

- We will argue later that if you want to improve safety performance, you must create the conditions in which safe *behavior* can and will occur, and Chapter 6 is devoted to this idea. Behavior and performance are tightly connected. But worker behavior is the *result* of leadership, culture, systems, and facility design—not the driver.

Leadership is really the heart of the matter. The third insight is this: *Elevating safety leadership is the most important single thing an organization can do to set improvement in motion.* Leadership is the place you want to go first, with the most energy that you can, and that will innervate all the rest of the things that influence good safety outcomes. What does that look like?

Safety leadership is an extremely broad subject area that we've written about at length in the book *Leading With Safety*.[i] Keeping that in mind, there are dimensions of safety leadership that stand out to us as the place every senior leader should start: the value for safety projected by a leader; the vision that leader holds for the organization; and the credibility the leader establishes behind both the value for safety and the safety vision. Certainly there are additional worthwhile safety leadership practices, but in our experience, these three are foundational.

PERSONAL VALUE FOR SAFETY

What does it mean for a leader to have a *personal value for safety*? As you think about this, think about the people around you,

How deep is your resolve?

How deep is your resolve to prevent injury and illness in your organization? What are you prepared to do? Do you:

- ❑ Learn the basics of organizational safety—how organizational factors produce safety excellence?
- ❑ Lead development of a safety strategy: objectives, methods, actions, and accountabilities?
- ❑ Understand the things your direct reports must do in order to reach safety objectives?
- ❑ Assess the culture of your organization for safety and for the organizational qualities that support safety?
- ❑ Assess the safety leadership capabilities of your direct reports. Require each report to have a measurable improvement plan?
- ❑ Develop leading and lagging indicators?
- ❑ Understand how to prevent Serious and Fatal Injuries?
- ❑ Understand the hazards present in your work environment and how they are mitigated?
- ❑ Understand the critical safety decision points within your organization?
- ❑ Engage with employees at all levels about safety issues?
- ❑ Have uncomfortable conversations, show emotions, and ask for honest feedback and what you can do to help. Receive difficult feedback gracefully?
- ❑ Select and promote employees who are safety leaders?

and ask yourself, does each one value safety? How important is safety to them—not because it's supposed to be important, not because somebody else says it's important, but how important is it *to them*? And how important is it *to you*? Really, and truly, deep down, how important is safety to you? How deep is your resolve to prevent injury and illness in your organization, in your community, and in your family?

If you think about the people who hold safety as a core value, they share some things in common. To the person, they believe they can make a difference. They believe they can be successful. They take responsibility for their decisions and actions. They are self-confident without having all the answers. They spend time learning about safety, injury causation, and prevention. And they know what it means to lose a loved one, or to suffer a debilitating injury or illness. We believe everyone has an intrinsic value for safety; that's just how we start, regardless of whatever competing values we may also hold. A deep personal value for safety is the appreciation, prioritization, and cultivation of that intrinsic value, and we find it develops over time, with experience, and with attention.

Leaders who embody a strong personal value for safety allocate resources, recognize contributions, talk about safety, and get personally involved. They hold themselves to the same high standards that they hold others to. They educate themselves, they look into issues, and they ask questions. They take action when they see someone in harm's way, and, crucially, they also take action on issues before bad things happen.

VISION FOR SAFETY

Of course, wanting something is not enough. To make something happen, we need a clear picture of what we are aiming for. Safety leaders need a *vision for safety*. By vision, we mean

How clear is your vision for safety?

How clear is your vision for safety? Can you paint a clear picture of what your organization will look like when you achieve the next level of performance? How many of the following statements accurately describe your vision?

- ☐ I can see specific methods to achieve the safety improvement we need.
- ☐ I can give at least 3 reasons why we must improve safety leadership, culture, and performance.
- ☐ I can see specific ways in which our organization needs to change in order to improve.
- ☐ I have safety data showing where we are now, and where we need to be in 5 years.
- ☐ I can describe the top 3 exposures that we must manage better.
- ☐ I can describe at least one new exposure that we will face in the next 3-5 years.
- ☐ I can name 3 behaviors which I and my direct reports must do with perfect reliability.
- ☐ I can name 3 behaviors which I want to see from every employee in my organization.
- ☐ My vision extends to contractors, suppliers, government, shareholders, and the general public.
- ☐ I can describe how this vision will benefit me, my family, shareholders, employees, and contractors.

knowing what it looks like as safety improves day by day. So yes, we want to get to zero safety incidents, but has the leader broken that down into small, achievable steps? Can the leader describe what people will be doing differently three, six, and nine months from now? What's going to change? How is that going to appear in our lives as employees at work? The effective safety leader can see that, can articulate it in a compelling way, can recognize progress as it's happening, and thus convince people around them that they can and will be successful.

Leaders who have a clear vision for safety talk about it. They talk about it frequently. They talk about it in some detail. They talk about it in concrete, practical terms. They bring it up in conversation, and they lead with it in formal presentations. They talk about it from the point of view of those around them, and show how everyone will benefit. We could go on about this for some time, but our point here is to convey the depth and richness of actions that result when a leader really has a well-developed vision.

CREDIBILITY

A good vision will challenge people's beliefs about what is possible, and it will ask some to reach outside their comfort zones. In order for a vision like this to be heard, a leader needs credibility with his or her constituents.

Credibility is formed when people know they can count on you for something. It is based on how people experience you, and what that experience tells them. Can people see the consistency between your words and actions? If you tell someone that you will do something, can they see that you did (or didn't) do it? If you say something is important to you, do they see you show it? When you are consistent in these ways, your credibility grows and trust deepens. People can predict, with great accuracy, what you will do. You begin to get the benefit of the doubt. And people will listen to you.

What culture are you creating?

Based on your actions, reactions, and inactions alone, is it in someone's best interest to:

Approach you	❑	or	❑	avoid you?
Report a problem	❑	or	❑	hide a problem?
Communicate openly	❑	or	❑	speak guardedly?
Collaborate with others	❑	or	❑	look after one's self?
Exceed expectations	❑	or	❑	comply minimally?
Take initiative	❑	or	❑	avoid responsibility?
Find room to improve	❑	or	❑	have all the answers?
Question flawed process	❑	or	❑	find workarounds?

When leaders are credible in the eyes of those around them, they do not have to work nearly as hard to influence people in their organizations. People are less resistant to change, need less convincing, and raise fewer objections. This does not mean there will be an absence of resistance, because resistance is a healthy and natural part of any organizational change, but people will spend less time testing "Is this for real?"

YOU ARE ALWAYS CREATING CULTURE

Notice that a leader's value, vision, and credibility are all established and conveyed through what the leader does day-to-day. This has major implications. We've all heard that leadership creates culture. And there's no doubt that is true.[ii] What we are saying is a little stronger than that: we're saying that leadership is *always* creating culture.

We'll explore culture in great detail in the next chapter, but for now take a few moments to think about your day-to-day interactions with people. Consider the content and tone of your e-mails, phone calls, face-to-face conversations, the questions you ask, the comments you make, and your body language when you meet with people. Think about what types of things you respond to and what types of things you don't respond to. Now try to imagine what others are taking away from these interactions. What are people learning from you about the best way to succeed in your organization?

Of course we want people to approach us, report problems, communicate openly, etc., and we hope that our actions, reactions, and inactions encourage such behaviors. Unfortunately, it doesn't matter what we intend to communicate if there's a gap between those intentions and what people actually take away from interactions directly with us, or even indirectly from others who are also interpreting us. What matters is what people see and what they experience when they interact with us and with our organization.

Note that you might not even be aware of the actions people are seeing, and you may not be aware of how people are seeing them. But the way you think about things—the things that you say, the things that you don't say, the way that you say it, the amount of emphasis that you give, your posture, your smile, your gestures—all of that 'stuff' matters. All of that stuff sends messages that people pick up and interpret. If you believe that safety incidents are inevitable, it's going to show. You can try to hide it, but if that's really what you think, it'll come through. It'll come through and it will affect the culture.

So when we say leaders are always creating culture, we don't mean that leaders are always *trying* to create culture. We don't mean that leaders are always *thinking* about the culture. We don't mean that leaders always have a program to work on their culture. Quite to the contrary, we mean that leaders are *always creating culture*, for better or for worse, whether they intend to or not.

If you want to improve safety, start with leadership and work from there. Have a vision for the safety culture you want to see at your organization. Put your values and credibility behind it. A shift in leadership can have immediate impact on performance. Safety systems, systems thinking, safe design, and safe behavior all flow from leadership. Impact on culture will be longer term. Your leadership will send some message about safety no matter what you do; why wouldn't that message be a credible one you really believe in?

REFERENCES

i Krause, T. (2005). *Leading With Safety*. Hoboken, NJ: Wiley.

ii Schein, E. H. (2010). *Organizational Culture and Leadership,* 4th ed. Hoboken, NJ: Wiley.

CHAPTER 4

CULTURE SUSTAINS PERFORMANCE — FOR BETTER OR FOR WORSE

We've never met a leader that didn't want a better culture for their organization. Statements like, "we need to change the culture," are heard every day in the life of a consultant. What is odd is that the leaders who make these statements usually think they are talking about other people, when in reality they are talking about themselves.

We know that "leadership creates culture;" any leader will tell you that. But oddly enough, "knowing" in this case doesn't reach very far. What is required is finding the connection between what I do as a leader and the kinds of cultural attributes I would like to change. Here is an example from Krause's experience:

> *I was the CEO of a growing global consulting firm. Doing projects for various types of organizations around the world required a great deal of flexibility. It wasn't enough to know how a project should be done in one location and industry; consultants needed to know how to work effectively in many different environments. They needed flexibility. Yet we were often criticized by clients on this very point. When we didn't win a project we often heard back, "You weren't flexible enough, we needed a partner that was flexible." We also heard that we could be arrogant in the way we talked about our work and the work of others.*
>
> *Hearing these things was frustrating to me. I was convinced that our methods were technically better than our competitors. We had done the research others hadn't, and we knew*

what worked and what didn't. There was no doubt in my mind that we were the best organization in the world at the kind of consulting we did. And I enjoyed saying so. In company meetings large and small, in conversations with colleagues, I loved to talk about how good we were and why.

What I didn't realize is the effect these statements were having on some employees. It tended to make them arrogant and inflexible. I was creating the same cultural attributes I wanted to change.

For leaders who want to change the culture of their organizations, this is the primary challenge: Find the connections between what you say, what you don't say, what decisions you make, what you emphasize, and the effect these things have on the culture of your organization.

Leadership stimulates growth and safety improvement in organizations; culture is the mechanism that sustains it. Culture will either reinforce the changes you've introduced or it will diminish them, depending on the values, beliefs, and behaviors that leaders have engrained in your organization. The fourth insight is that *leadership stimulates safety improvement, but culture sustains performance.*

To say that culture is critically important is not to diminish the role of safety systems. In fact, an organization that doesn't have good safety systems will find it extremely difficult to develop a strong safety culture. This is because leaders who really value safety will learn that safety systems are critically important and they will put them in place.

Organizational leaders who don't have this insight may want a great safety culture, but not realize that you can't fake it. Giving lip service to safety undermines safety culture.

DEFINING CULTURE

To understand this insight, let's first explain what we mean by 'culture.' It is often taken for granted because the concept seems so obvious and so powerful, but few people realize the context in which organizational culture exists. Indeed, it didn't emerge as a subject of inquiry until 1960, and it didn't become prominent until after 1985. Organizational culture as we understand it started with Edgar Schein's observations in the late 1950s.[i]

Schein was working for National Training Labs in Boston, doing leaderless training groups, also called 'T' groups. Schein and his colleagues were interested in how business leaders acted in groups. Specifically, they wanted to know how authority was related to leadership, how employees decided to follow (or not), and what leaders did to gain informal authority.

Schein would bring a group of executives in for several days of training and he would begin by assembling the group, sitting down with them in a circle, and saying nothing. When people finally asked what was going on, he would answer with a question: What do you want to be going on? And then he would be silent.

What followed was very interesting: People would begin to structure the activities of the group. Leaders would emerge and standards would start to be set. Some individuals were angry, some were having fun, others perplexed. But it didn't take long for the group to begin to develop ways of doing things, and out of this came a sense of group identity, a set of unwritten rules for how things would be done, and an informal designation of leaders. A culture of the organization had been born, often within a few days. Schein named these sets of behaviors "organizational culture" and began to study and write about it. When learning about the organizations he was consulting with, it was of primary importance.

In a formal sense, *culture* is now defined as the shared values, beliefs, and assumptions that govern behavior. Informally, culture is expressed as "the way we do things around here." Even though most people have heard and understand these definitions, culture can be difficult to pin down because values, beliefs, and assumptions are not directly observable, and "the way we do things" is too vague to be useful. In the book *Leading with Safety*, we present a set of measures, drawn from the research literature, that characterize an organization's culture and safety climate. These characteristics turn out to be excellent leading indicators of safety as well as organizational performance in general. With them, we can measure specific cultural attributes that predict safe behavior and which correlate statistically with injury frequency.

TWO TYPES OF CULTURE CHARACTERISTICS

These characteristics of culture break down into two broad categories. One category is called '*safety climate*' or sometimes '*safety culture;*' it has to do with how people talk and act with respect to safety. It asks, "In this organization, do we value safety? Do managers, supervisors, and workers all act in ways that demonstrate that worker safety is actually important?"

The other category has to do with *organizational functioning* in general. It describes the kinds of relationships that motivate people to contribute their best efforts. It is supported by a large and robust body of published research that shows that trusting, reciprocal relationships between employees, between employees and their supervisors, and between employees and the organization all contribute to a positive working environment and high levels of organizational functioning. Higher organizational functioning, in turn, leads to better engagement, more teamwork, loyalty, and people investing discretionary time, effort, and enthusiasm in their work.

This idea of social reciprocity is an important one for organizations. An employee who is part of a culture endowed with this characteristic has the sense that, "This organization and the people in it care about me. I feel supported. I am seen as a person who matters. I am recognized." And the more people feel that, the more they reciprocate by doing really fine work, going the extra mile, being committed, being engaged with the work, and all those other good things.

On the other hand, when organizational functioning is low, trust and communication are compromised. People feel insecure, or even threatened, and they respond by protecting their own interests. If I think, "This is an organization that doesn't care about me, that doesn't support me, that isn't really on my side," then my next thought is, "Tell me what time I'm supposed to leave and I'm leaving. Tell me the minimum I have to do to get by, and that's what I'll be doing." And why wouldn't I?

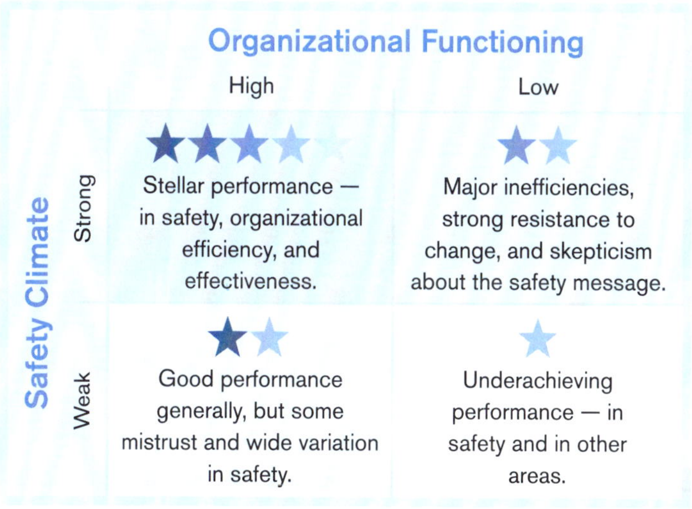

Figure 6

ORGANIZATIONAL FUNCTIONING AND SAFETY CLIMATE COMBINE TO INFLUENCE BEHAVIOR AND PERFORMANCE

Organizational functioning and safety climate interact with each other in ways that affect decisions, safety-related behavior, and performance. As summarized in the figure on the previous page, high organizational functioning stokes the motivation to perform, while a positive safety climate focuses people on what's important. And of course the inverse is also true: Low organizational functioning drains motivation, and a weak safety climate scatters focus. We'll explore the interactions of safety climate and organizational functioning using three case studies.

CASE STUDY 1:
Strong Safety Climate, High Organizational Functioning

The client was the senior leadership team of an oil refinery that was preparing to shut down. The refinery was among the biggest employers in the area, and its employees knew that their jobs would be gone in 24 months. Refinery leaders had the very challenging job of not only retaining employees, but keeping them safe and fully engaged during an extended period of stress.

The senior management team decided to accomplish this by focusing on the safety and well-being of their people. Their vision was to close the refinery, "Proud that we maintained safe, environmentally sound and reliable operations; proud that we treated people fairly; and proud of my personal contribution, growth, and development." In order to create an environment in which every employee knew they were valued and cared for, and where the attention to safe work practices was paramount, this senior-level team committed to practicing and measuring their own critical safety leadership behaviors.

Their unwavering commitment to their vision was evidenced by continuous improvement in their own leadership practices, which steadily increased over the two years. And that commitment paid off: The refinery closed its doors with the safest, most reliable, and most productive record in its history, and every employee who wanted a job had one waiting. This refinery and its leadership team epitomize high organizational functioning coupled with a strong safety climate.

CASE STUDY 2:
Weak Safety Climate, High Organizational Functioning

The picture changes significantly when organizational functioning is high but safety climate is weak. In these organizations, people are committed to their work and put in all kinds of discretionary effort, but they act in highly unpredictable ways when it comes to safety. An employee might feel loyal to their boss and workgroup, and believe that the best way to demonstrate that is to protect their safety numbers and hide the fact that they were injured on the job. Or perhaps a leader might feel loyal to the organization, and believe the best way to demonstrate that is to lose no productivity and keep the machines running at all costs, even if it means failing to address critical safety issues.

This unpredictable approach to safety is essentially what happened at NASA leading up to the Space Shuttle Columbia failure. The Columbia Accident Investigation Board reported that the cause of the failure was as much from a broken safety culture as it was from a technical problem. Individuals within NASA had recognized the risk of losing insulating foam from the external fuel tanks of the space shuttle. They knew that loss of foam could destroy the mission. They knew that a hazard like that meant, "Don't fly." Yet NASA flew anyway, because the people who knew about the problem were at the middle of the organization, and the right information didn't flow to the top.

We were invited to work with the agency-wide senior leadership team helping NASA strengthen their safety climate and culture. NASA needed to understand how and why information did not flow up to the right people. Meetings offered powerful opportunities to witness communication and thereby observe culture in action. So we observed a lot of meetings. NASA *ran* on meetings. NASA seemed to have more meetings than anybody, and the meetings we observed had a distinctive protocol. Attendees met in large rooms with a rectangular table at the center seating about 12 people. Most of those 12 people were people whose names you would recognize. Then there were 50 or so lower-ranking people seated in multiple rows around the periphery. The hierarchy was unambiguous. A meeting like this one would determine whether a shuttle mission would receive the green light or not. The 12 people in the center would make that decision. The atmosphere in the room would be highly charged and very tense.

It was almost combative. When two people disagreed, it was very likely there would be a winner and a loser; it was very unlikely that there would be a difference of opinion between good people and then a dialog. So if you were a 30-year old engineer and you had been studying the properties of insulating foam on external fuel tanks, and you were sitting at the edge of the room, and there was about to be a decision to fly or not fly—you were required to stand up and say, "Doctor Famous, my data show something quite different and I really think you ought to reconsider the decision that you're about to make." That's what it would take. A 30-year old engineer would have to put herself on the line in order to be heard, and do so on issues that she believed were of vital importance to those in the center of the room. NASA is filled with extraordinary people who are deeply committed to the Agency's work and who would speak out for issues perceived to be mission-critical. But unless the value for safety is just as palpable, unless safety is also seen as mission-critical, unless the 12 people in the center of the room are known to want safety issues raised, it is unlikely a 30-year old engineer would risk her reputation for it.

Turning this around at NASA was surprisingly easy. Leaders needed to recognize how their behaviors impacted the culture, and not just when they were promoting safety, but in their day-to-day interactions. NASA did several things in an effort to build this awareness of behavior and its impact, but there is a simple exercise that anyone can do. Find a colleague you trust—or hire someone. Remove from your email anything that you don't want to share. Then go through your mailbox together, talk about each message, and talk through alternative responses. Imagine how different responses would impact people's beliefs about you, their beliefs about the organization, and their future behavior. How often do you receive a message that makes you angry or frustrated? How often does a message leave you feeling empowered or supported? How you respond in a simple email has cultural effects that radiate throughout the organization, but you'll likely find that responding well is much easier said than done. A commitment to safety excellence demands we are sensitive to the impact day-to-day behaviors have on culture.

CASE STUDY 3:
Strong Safety Climate, Low Organizational Functioning

NASA had strong organizational functioning and a weaker safety climate. What happens when safety climate is strong but organizational functioning is weak? We see this in many large corporations that are deeply committed to safety. Geographic dispersion, complex organizational structures, and bureaucratic systems all strain organizational functioning, which is why large corporations often struggle with it. When these same corporations value safety, they devote immense resources to safety training, tracking safety metrics, and developing procedures. In these organizations, we see senior managers working extremely hard to get their safety messages out there.

This all sounds great for safety, but the weakness in organizational functioning creates all kinds of hurdles for leaders who are trying to do the right thing. These organizations suffer from a lack of trust between levels and across organizational boundaries. There are big silos. In one organization we worked with, an outdated forced-rank performance management system kept people so busy protecting their own interests that there was little trust between co-workers. Communications were politicized. When something went wrong, people would blame others to protect themselves. People invested hours every day creating paper trails and defensive documentation.

This weak organizational functioning creates drag on safety (and everything else). We once attended a three-day off-site safety conference for employees who had served on a safety committee for one division of a large oil and gas company. Employees from all over the world had been flown in. The conference started off with speeches from two corporate executives, the division president, and the division safety manager. As we observed the scene, we couldn't believe the time, attention, and resources being devoted to safety. But as we looked more closely, we saw people rolling their eyes as the executives spoke. These were safety volunteers rolling their eyes at executives talking about *safety*!

Later, we asked what that was all about, and we were told that employees were cynical. They were hearing political speeches, not safety messages. The messages sounded mechanical to them. This organization did have extraordinary safety performance, but they seemed to be accomplishing it at an astronomical cost. Given the degree of distrust that we observed, we were not surprised to learn that the company was not performing well in other areas: Weak organizational functioning was taking its toll.

Turning around low organizational functioning is particularly challenging when that functioning is impeded by bureaucracy. It requires that leaders find ways to encourage critical thinking, reward good judgment, make people feel seen and heard, and recognize them as individuals whose ideas matter. If existing systems prevent this from happening, those systems have to be modified—sometimes torn down and rebuilt—in order for real change to occur.

SUMMARY

Culture sustains performance. And like Edgar Schein who pioneered the study of organizational culture, we assert that leaders should not focus on culture alone: Culture is improved by focusing on real business issues, and there is no better place to start than safety.

When organizational functioning is high and the safety climate is strong, people step up and contribute to safety in really effective ways. Team leads don't just grab a generic pre-job safety briefing off the internet five minutes before they need it and read it to their team in a monotone voice; no, they invest the time and creativity to prepare an informative briefing on a relevant topic and practice until they can communicate it effectively. This same commitment to excellence is seen in other areas that are clearly valued by the organization. The high levels of trust make change implementations more efficient, and the strong communication and teamwork yield higher levels of organizational effectiveness.

The next chapter provides the foundation for strengthening the safety climate and organizational culture through safe decision-making. It offers an understanding of core safety concepts that will not only help leaders create the right climate around safety, but also point to effective prevention strategies.

REFERENCES

i Schein, E. H., & Bennis, W. G. (1965). *Personal and organizational change through group methods: The laboratory approach.* New York: Wiley.

CHAPTER 5

LEADING SAFETY STARTS WITH UNDERSTANDING SAFETY

The fifth insight is this: *All safety leaders need to understand core safety concepts.*

A lot of organizations suffer a disconnect between safety professionals and other leaders. Operational leaders are paid to assess situations and make decisions aggressively. They work in cycles of what is wrong and what it will take to fix it, and they are good at what they do. However, this drive can prove counterproductive to safety performance and improvement when it's not grounded in a solid understanding of safety fundamentals. It surprises safety professionals to learn how often core safety concepts are misunderstood or unknown to leaders at various levels throughout an organization, and indeed that knowledge gap generally expands as you go up. It is important for all parties to realize that safety is not necessarily intuitive—but there is no reason it can't be learned and taught.

We once worked on a safety improvement project with a refinery in Louisiana. The effort was driven by a steering committee comprised of front-line employees, requiring little from site management except allocation of time to the workers. Over a period of two years the steering committee developed a first-rate safety improvement process, engaging workers and getting results. Awareness was high, behaviors were improving, and teams were finding work reconfiguration projects and executing them well. The safety numbers were coming down consistently, and they were statistically significant. It was a model project.

Then, over a two month period they had a number of incidents, seemingly out of the blue. The steering committee tested for statistical significance and concluded the incidents were due to normal variation. They looked at leading indicators and found no basis for alarm or re-direction of their efforts. The best decision they could make was to stay the course.

But a new plant manager saw the increased numbers and pushed the panic button. It looked to him like the program he was taking credit for was suddenly faltering. In truth, he knew virtually nothing about the program and his relationship to safety was no more sophisticated than looking at the end point numbers. When the numbers went down he ignored safety, and when they went up he propelled himself into action.

He made the decision—without consulting with the steering committee—that the number of safety observations must go up, and the way he would ensure that was tying an observation goal to a financial incentive. He thought he was taking the action needed to address a problem decisively. But he was actually destroying the hard work and spent resources of two years of work.

Why was this disastrous decision made? The plant manager fundamentally didn't understand how safety works. He failed to see the role of employee engagement, the way the improvement process was working to improve the safety of the workplace, and the meaning of the data on number of injuries. He wasn't a bad person and he wasn't a fool. He just didn't understand and, most destructively, he didn't know what he still needed to learn.

Unfortunately, this story is not as rare as we would hope. It happens frequently. An aggressive manager moving up the chain sees the plant manager role as a stepping stone, wants to make a mark, and suffers from over-confidence bias (See Chapter 7 on bias). To many safety pros, the situation is pure frustration. It should be seen as an opportunity for improvement.

CORE SAFETY CONCEPT 1:

A safe workplace is much more than awareness.

A few years ago we were working with a VP of Operations at a mid-sized oil and gas company. The VP was well intended, and he sincerely wanted to show his commitment to safety. However, the entirety of his safety leadership plan was to send a message out to all his employees every two weeks. In each message, he'd tell a story about an incident he'd heard about, and the moral of the story was a *Hill-Street-Blues*-esque, "Let's be careful out there." He believed that if people were aware of the risks they were facing, that then they would protect themselves. He believed that safety was mainly a matter of using common sense. He believed raising awareness was the most powerful thing he could do to help his group improve in safety.

Now this executive was not stupid. He was a man we knew to be of high integrity and intelligence. He had come up through his organization without operations experience, and he was simply uninformed—severely—about how safety works. We thought about what we might say that would be helpful to him. This is the predicament many safety professionals are in. It caused us to want to write this book.

Awareness of risk is important in safety. But it is a small piece in a complex puzzle. To make the workplace safer, *you actually have to make the workplace safer.* Getting new awareness will help for a short time, but an awareness campaign that ignores the state of the workplace ultimately does more harm than good. It contributes to a culture of cynicism, which is not uncommon in the workplace today. Workers think: "I'm supposed to 'be more aware,' and they ask me to work in an environment that is obviously unsafe. I turn in problems and never hear back. Then we have a safety contest."

We have observed that organizations that think awareness alone is enough to improve safety often try to achieve those gains through incentives, like the new plant manager in the beginning of this chapter. Let's be clear: Making financial reward contingent on safety results is almost always a mistake. It sends the wrong message, fails to address the real issues, and causes the culture to deteriorate. When you make pay contingent on safety outcomes, without ensuring healthy systems, processes, tools, practices, and leadership necessary to drive those outcomes, then you're basically relying on awareness of the importance of safety to drive results. You're hoping that if people are aware that safety is part of their job, and worth paying for, then they can and will do all the right things to avoid getting hurt. All that awareness still needs support and action to make a safer workplace.

CORE SAFETY CONCEPT 2:

Injuries are prevented by a safe workplace. A safe workplace includes safe decision making; proper design, equipment, and facilities; excellent safety systems and work processes; safety leadership; and safe behavior.

If any one of these factors is sub-standard, your organization is exposed to injuries. The solution is not to chase down every hazard, but to develop mechanisms that create safe workplaces. Those mechanisms need to address the workplace as a whole because the parts interact with each other. For example, if an instrument panel is designed poorly, the operator can usually work around it. But if the worker is distracted *and* the instrument panel is designed poorly, the combination of poor design and at-risk behavior results in an incident. Any one sub-standard aspect of the workplace can become a precursor to an incident—including a serious injury or a fatality—and multiple aspects can combine to escalate that risk.

CORE SAFETY CONCEPT 3:

The safety of a workplace held constant will produce a variable number of incidents.

Variation in safety incident numbers is both entirely expected and not inherently meaningful. A constant level of safety in a given workplace will always produce a variable number of safety incidents. The reason is that random variation is high in workplace safety. Some days the noise level and poorly written procedures can be compensated for by safe behavior. Other days they can't. There is a chance factor, not in how safe the workplace is but in how many incidents happen from a given situation. That may sound reasonable when you hear it, but in practice it proves easy to forget. In fact, the higher up we go in an organization, the more of an issue this becomes. Senior leaders want to look at outcomes, not processes and predictors. In safety, outcomes are numbers of incidents. This is fine if we understand the nature of the distribution of incidents and the inevitability of variation. But if leaders don't understand this basic concept, they will inevitably make bad safety decisions.

Statistical analysis can help us understand variation. Say you had 36 injuries in a year at your plant. You averaged three per month. You intuitively know that you did not have three injuries each and every month. That kind of consistency would be weird, quite frankly. Weird like a basketball team finishing every game in every season with the exact same score.

So, if this is your company and 36 of your employees are injured over a year, what does it mean when you have a month like July with zero injuries? Does that mean we had an inherently safer workplace in July compared to other months? Maybe. Maybe not. Statistically, the number zero in a month when three is the average is not compelling evidence of improvement. In the same way, the number five or six in a given month doesn't mean you did anything to make safety worse. But because it is human nature to look for patterns and try to make meaning even with limited data, it's very easy to see that zero people were injured in July, while six people were injured in October, and come up with plausible explanations in hindsight.

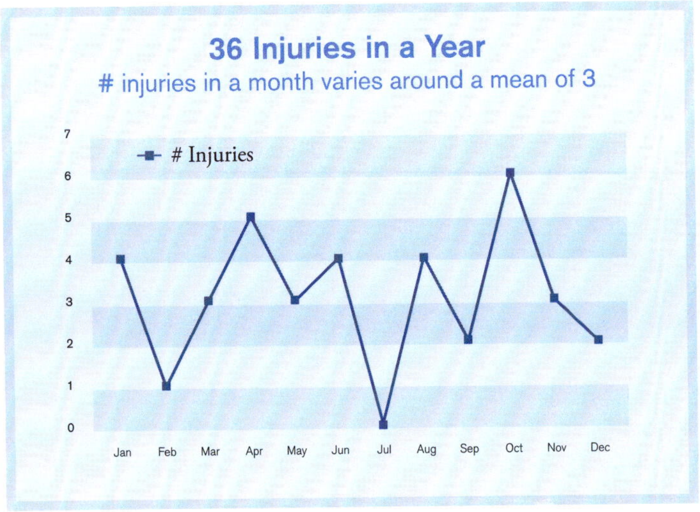

Figure 7

For example, suppose you focus on the 'spikes' and then attribute them to a new piece of equipment purchased in October and a lighter workload in July. If you believe these explanations to be true—and you probably would, if you're like most of us—then they would inform your reactions. You might send your operators off for extra training next time you install new equipment, or you might send all of your safety professionals to a conference next time the schedule looks light.

But while you were busy interpreting individual data points, something else was happening altogether: Perhaps underneath all of the variation in the past year was a theme related to the experience of your workforce. For instance, when the most experienced members of your workforce were present, your injury rate went down; when your workers with less experience were present, more people were hurt. Had you known this, you would never pull experienced safety professionals or operators off the floor for training or any kind of professional development without first ensuring that experienced workers and supervisors were present for every shift. Unfortunately, it is extremely common in organizations for leaders to focus on a single data point in hindsight, overreact, and take the wrong action.

Distinguish special-cause and common-cause variation.

In the same way that W. Edwards Deming used statistical process control (SPC) charts to understand variation in quality metrics, you can use SPC and a few simple decision rules to understand the variation in your safety data. When you see six people injured in October and want to dig deeper, an SPC chart will tell you where to look. It will tell you if you need to look at October specifically, or if you should look at what's been happening all along. Deming called this the difference between special-cause and common-cause variation, and it is something every senior leader ought to be able to distinguish.

Common-cause variation consists of noise and other unmanaged exposures. In the example above, worker experience is the common-cause variation: It is a factor throughout the dataset. Special-cause variation consists of short-term changes in exposure. If the plant was closed for three weeks in a month and there were zero injuries, it's probably because exposure was minimal while the plant was closed.

SPC charts use the knowledge that in a set of normally distributed observations, nearly all (99.7%) of the data will fall within three standard deviations of their mean. Deming defined this as *common-cause variation*. Data falling outside of three standard deviations are interpreted as if they belong to a different distribution, what Deming called *special-cause variation*. The limits of common-cause variation are represented on our graph by a pair of bounding orange lines. The decision rule for our plant with 36 injuries is this: In Figure 8, if any point falls outside the orange lines, investigate what happened that particular month. If not, as happens to be the case here, investigate what is happening across the whole year.

CORE SAFETY CONCEPT 4:

Leading indicators and longitudinal root cause analysis give a more complete picture of workplace safety than incident numbers.

We can't rely on outcome data alone to tell us about the safety of the workplace. You could cut exposure by 30% in a quarter and your injury rate may still go up. You could let exposure creep up by 10 or 15% in a quarter, and your injury rate could go down. Injuries and exposure never track perfectly.

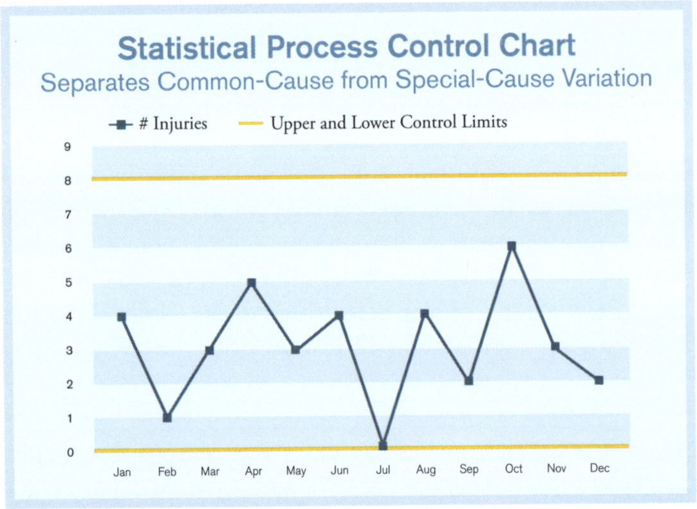

Figure 8

These days, organizations are trying to develop tools to understand how well they are creating safe work places. Organizations that are good at safety tend to have comprehensive safety management systems, and safety leaders should be looking at measures of the effectiveness and reliability of those systems. Organizations that are good at safety also use a variety of other leading indicators; safety leaders should be asking for valid and reliable measures of culture, leadership, and behavior.

Specifically, safety leaders should be using leading indicators that have a demonstrable relationship to safety performance, including: safety leadership best practices, response time to safety issues, improvement in critical safety behaviors, the percentage of the workforce actively participating in safety, and quality of incident investigations. These are the "vital signs" of their organizations. Together, they give a more complete picture of workplace safety than outcome data alone.

Use longitudinal analysis to identify improvement opportunities.

Chasing hazards can be an exercise in frustration without visible benefits. An incident tells us we need to fix something, then another something else, then something else again, and yet we continue to have incidents without seeing a significant downward trend. A tool that can provide leverage is longitudinal root cause analysis. It reveals *systemic exposure.* What we mean by systemic exposure is the exposure that is there all the time—the exposure responsible for the common-cause variation in your injury data. We want to understand it by longitudinal root cause analysis because looking at a group of root cause analyses together lets you identify the themes that run across the series. Those themes might take the form of failing to anticipate issues that will arise during work, or not responding to issues until after an incident occurs, or just low quality incident investigations.

The senior leader who looks at Figure 8 might be tempted to focus on the six individual incidents that happened in October, because that is the worst month all year. But a quick look at the

SPC chart for that year suggests that one or more common causes is at play. Knowing that, the leader needs to use longitudinal root cause analysis to identify exposure, examining not one but the last 30 root cause analyses to look for systemic issues that cut across them.

If you only hunt for causes going case by case, your work flow looks something like this: You investigate one incident at a time, do your root cause analysis, find some stuff, fix what you can, and close out the report. These individual analyses matter, but it's a very slow way to work. On the other hand, if you look at a whole series of analyses, identify themes across them, and address those themes, you will get at systemic exposure much more effectively and see some immediate lift. Maybe equipment is wearing out slowly over time and maintenance issues are not being prioritized correctly – this would show up as a gradual trend in data. Or maybe there is a culture of "get 'er done" which causes people to jump into their work without anticipating what could go wrong. This would show up as a lot of seemingly random variation in the data. Or maybe the analysis reveals that there are leaders in the organization who are much better than others at anticipating safety issues, getting their workers to recognize and respond to the issues, verifying that the issues get resolved, etc. This would show up as significant differences in injury rates between departments or functions.

Injuries result from exposure to hazards, which come in a plethora of forms and may act in isolation or combine. Some will occur as singular events, but many hazards are common and ongoing. Creating a safer workplace is a matter of effective analysis, and the injury causation analysis and prevention strategy is twofold: (1) Use statistical analysis to distinguish between common-cause and special-cause variation; and (2) Get a more complete picture of exposure using a variety of metrics and longitudinal root-cause analysis.

It is common for leaders to react before they have enough information. Their intentions are noble, but bad analysis only makes things worse. You need to appreciate the complexity with which hazards may interact and know when to take the long view. Testing for statistical significance will start you in the right direction. Injury causation analysis directs those best of intentions to strategies where they can really do some good.

CORE SAFETY CONCEPT 5:

The precursors to serious injuries and fatalities tend to be fundamentally different from the precursors to minor injuries.

As discussed in Chapter 2, the Safety Triangle can be traced back to Herbert William Heinrich's 1931 book *Industrial Accident Prevention, A Scientific Approach*,[i] and a series of ratios that became known as Heinrich's Law. Heinrich suggested that for every major injury, there are 29 accidents causing minor injuries and 300 accidents resulting in no injuries at all. Working from the observation that accidents tend to share common root causes, the Safety Triangle became a popular visualization for how preventing accidents with minor consequences could effectively prevent the same accidents causing serious injuries.

The Safety Triangle is no longer the predominant view in the safety field, and we need to reexamine the ideas tied to it. For instance, the first book written by one of us (Krause) included the statement, "80-95% of unsafe behaviors are caused by at-risk behavior."[1] This is a misleading statement out of context

1. That observation is often abbreviated from its original passage. What we said was this: "The unsafe behaviors in question are the work practices of the facility. In a majority of cases – from 80% to 95% – accidents are caused by un-safe behavior. This statement emphatically does not mean that the injury is the employee's fault ... Wherever it appears in this book, the statement that 80% to 95% of accidents are caused by unsafe behavior refers to a very specific kind of cause known as the final common pathway."

and needs to be dropped from the way we talk about safety causation. The mistake is understandable; if you look at a series of incidents and ask what their "cause" was, you'll see lots of worker behavior on the surface. But if you look deeper, you'll see that the behavioral factors are usually related to decisions made by supervisors, managers, and senior leaders. Perhaps you see that a worker failed to follow the procedure and stood in the wrong place. The other worker didn't see her and moved the vehicle, crushing and killing the worker. That scenario looks like the workers' behavior caused the incident, but the picture is incomplete. What isn't seen is that management knew the procedure was flawed, had planned to address it, but had not followed through; the work being done was incentivized for speed (a decision that was made without regard for its obvious implications); and the supervisor had failed to do a required JSA prior to the job being started.

What we have thought and taught for 40 years is that smaller injuries lead to bigger injuries, reducing smaller injuries would necessarily reduce larger ones, and unsafe behaviors are the primary cause of injuries. None of these concepts turn out to be true. We do indeed see a distribution where there are more minor incidents and fewer major incidents; but when we are able to impact how many minor incidents occur, it does not directly correlate to a change in major incidents. If we want to address serious injuries and fatalities, we must focus on them as a special class with special characteristics.

What this means for injury causation is that senior leaders need information about the root causes and precursors to serious injuries and fatalities separately from that of other kinds of incidents. Longitudinal root-cause analyses should look for patterns in the entire group of incidents, and for patterns that are unique to SIFs. For example, when we assisted a fertilizer manufacturer with a longitudinal root cause analysis for SIFs, the analysis revealed that a simple behavior such as "eyes on path" was just as likely to be associated with a SIF as with a non-SIF; meanwhile a safety management system failure such as a pre-task risk assessment being completed in a superficial manner was much more likely to be associated with a SIF. The implication for senior leaders was clear: They needed to understand their safety management systems better, and pay at least as much attention to how well their safety systems were functioning as they were already paying to worker behavior.

SUMMARY

As managers, we believe in taking responsibility for our decisions and actions, and we believe in learning from the past to prevent serious incidents in the future. We do not accept that injuries are beyond our control, nor should we. But when leaders assume month-to-month variation in injury frequency is due to month-to-month changes in workplace safety level, without testing that assumption, they introduce noise into the system. When leaders attribute improvement to a particular program without adequate data, or attribute failure to "someone who should have done better" without understanding the real situation, they are doing more harm than good.

So, once a safety leader understands these core concepts, how will their safe decisions and behaviors change?

- Stop chasing hazards and start developing systems that improve the safety of the workplace.
- Focus on SIFs as a starting point. Work from the top of the triangle down, rather than the bottom up.
- Don't waste time on awareness campaigns. Put that time into improving systems.
- Stop over-reacting to variation in incident rates. Start using statistical analysis to find trends in your data.

- Develop leading indicators and use longitudinal analysis to find trends.

Safety leaders need to start having conversations about these core concepts and assure that they are understood at all levels of the organization. They are not understood widely at the present, even in organizations that have good performance. A critical role of the safety professional is to facilitate this education.

REFERENCES

i Heinrich, H. W. (1941) *Industrial accident prevention*, a scientific approach. New York: McGraw-Hill Book Company.

CHAPTER 6

THE ROLE OF BEHAVIOR IN ORGANIZATIONAL SAFETY

Twenty-five years ago, Krause, Hidley, and Hodson published a book called *The Behavior-Based Safety Process*.[i] In that book we made the statement: "80-95% of incidents are caused by unsafe behavior."[1] The idea that behavior can be a contributing cause of incidents is correct, but it is also misleading. It sets up a leader to think, "If we just fix these employees, most of our incidents will go away." It can encourage the leader to place blame inappropriately. And it can get the leader off the hook of being responsible for creating a safer workplace. The use of this phrase and the variety of conflicting opinions about it has muddied the water concerning something very important in safety: the role of behavior in incident causation and prevention. In this chapter we will provide clarification about this important issue.

The insight that safety leaders need to understand is this: *Incidents are caused by a network of factors including design, safety systems, leadership, culture, and behavior.* The role of behavior in incident causation is important, but it is only one piece, and usually a small one at that. Focusing on behavior as if it is the whole story is a serious mistake. It can alienate employees, drive accurate data underground, and leave other risk factors unchecked. For all these reasons, understanding the role of behavior is essential to good safety leadership.

The word "behavior" has different meanings to different people. For the labor leader it may conjure up thoughts of workers being blamed unfairly, and through the misapplication of the term "BBS" they've had good reason to arrive at this association. In the behavioral sciences, the word "behavior" signals a way to understand human activity by using the scientific method. It is usually a positive word for organizational leaders, but it gets to specific actions of critical importance.

Most leaders, when they talk about behavior, are thinking of front-line employee behavior. The person that got hurt did something that caused the incident. Look at the last ten incidents in your organization. Examine the incident reports, and you'll see the role of behavior jumping off the page. The conclusion will often say something like, "instruct employee in safe procedures," and the cause of the incident will often be shown as the employee's failure to follow a procedure. But these elements don't tell the whole story. In fact, their omissions tell a misleading story. The behavior of leaders all the way to the CEO and the Board are actually implicated in incident causation. We'll give examples of this shortly, but first we need to clarify some aspects of "behavior-based safety."

A BRIEF HISTORY OF BEHAVIOR-BASED SAFETY

The first researcher to use applied behavior analysis was Dr. Judi Komaki. Her seminal studies published in 1978-79 along with the early work of Proctor and Gamble were the references Krause drew from when he first began to consult with organizations on safety improvement. P&G used the phrase "behavior-based safety" to describe the work Gene Earnest and Jim Palmer were doing within their organization and, to our knowledge, that's where the term was coined.

This early work was ground-breaking in that it showed that safety-related behaviors could be operationally defined and measured. Measurement made it possible to evaluate new safety efforts. However, this early work lacked a mechanism to tie behaviors to their real causes, as we'll discuss in this chapter.

In 1990, when we first described the behavior-based safety process, we outlined four key steps: First, identify and define safety critical behaviors; second, gather data through observation; third, give feedback; and finally, *use the accumulated data to identify, prioritize, and solve problems standing in the way of a safe work place.*

We designed this process to incorporate the range of factors connected to at-risk behavior in the workplace. The first three steps were straight up applied behavioral analysis. But the fourth step was a deliberate attempt to recognize that behavior itself, while a useful tool and important factor, was not the whole of the issue. Our method aggregated data on at-risk behavior and used it to find opportunities to make the workplace safer. If workers aren't following a procedure, why not? Is the behavior within their control? Is the work designed properly? Does the culture support doing it safely or does no one follow the procedure? Most importantly, what needs to be done to set the stage for safe behavior? We taught front-line workers, supervisors, and managers a methodology to understand behavioral data as a guide to finding the most pressing places to address facility, safety system, culture, and leadership issues.

Many companies took this on enthusiastically and developed dozens of safety action plans for making the workplace safer. Senior leaders got involved to support and provide resources, and to do so promptly and effectively. Often a metric was established that measured how many safe action plans were being completed, and that metric turned out to be a predictor of safety improvement. The whole process of defining and observing behaviors culminated in a safer workplace. Many of those organizations today can give years of examples where this was done and where employee engagement improved, culture improved, incident rates declined, and the workplace got safer.

The cultural change wasn't small. Many senior leaders told us, after three to five years of doing the BBS described above, that they were pleased to have improved safety like they had set out to do, but that what surprised and delighted them was the profound cultural change that followed (see Chapter 4 on culture).

BBS DEFINITION MUDDIED IN THE MARKETPLACE

However, as behavior-based safety became more popular, some organizations started doing it on their own, and some very large corporations, without understanding what BBS actually was, began to mandate that every business unit have a "behavior-based safety process." Demand for behavior-based safety was very high and consultants came along to compete for the business. The competition was very good for us: We were market leaders, and our desire to continue to lead compelled us to do our best work and continue to innovate. But this made us expensive, and some other consulting firms readily recognized the opportunity to compete on price. Dropping the fourth element made it very easy to cut consulting costs: It appeared to save everyone time, money, and hassle. After all, isn't behavior-based safety mainly about observing people and giving feedback? The answer is an emphatic "no," but not enough people understood this, and the term BBS was used to label approaches even when they failed to incorporate the crucial fourth step that takes an organization beyond feedback to deep problem solving.

Some groups short-cut it even more, marketing incentive programs and other awareness programs that did nothing to improve workplace safety, as if they were BBS-supported. Some labor leaders objected to behavior-based safety in general. They failed to distinguish between those approaches that made the workplace safer and the knock-offs and copy-cats that skipped some steps (or made up new ones). Labor's complaint, that it is wrong-headed to blame the employee, was an accurate criticism for some approaches, but inaccurate for others. What should have happened at that point (and what should happen now) is for labor and consultant representatives to get together and figure out a way to keep the best of actual BBS while avoiding the pitfalls. Several attempts have been made to do this, but success above the site level has been limited, mainly because of political considerations.

Unfortunately for the safety community, the distinction between BBS and other practitioners that claim the same name has never been sufficiently clear. To this day you can find labor organizations that condemn what they've come to know as BBS, even though huge numbers of facilities they represent use the actual BBS practices quite successfully. Most leading companies have ignored the noise all this and jockeying created, and proceeded on their own lights to do what they think is right for safety.

Although labor can be rightly criticized for its role in perpetuating all this confusion, they were certainly right about some things. They were right that if you started with the word 'behavior' as the focal point of a safety improvement effort, you stood a fair chance of misdirecting attention primarily to workers. They were right that one effect of this would be massive effort aimed at small injuries while major risks were not looked at sufficiently. And they were right that an approach that emphasized the narrow version of behavior could easily miss the importance of serious injuries and fatalities. Properly done BBS efforts also impact serious injuries and fatalities, because they require an observation strategy that is focused on precursors and which consequently gives priority to situations and activities that have high risk for serious and fatal events.

DECISION MAKING INFLUENCES BEHAVIOR

On December 9, 2010, a dust explosion killed three employees and seriously injured another at a metal recycling facility. On the day of the explosion, a maintenance worker installed a bad blade in a blending machine and returned it to service. Soon after he started the machine, a flash fire developed inside it, and the machine exploded. This initial explosion ignited dust which had accumulated inside the building and caused a second, catastrophic explosion. So yes, an action by the maintenance employee—installing a bad blade in the machine and returning it to service—*was* the last thing that anyone did to contribute to the incident. Let's be clear: Knowing that is what happened is crucial to understanding the event. But let's also be clear on this: What the worker did is only the endpoint of the story, not the actual cause of the event. Knowing the result, without knowing the causes that led to it, reveals almost no useful information about what needs to be done to prevent this kind of event from happening again.

When things go wrong in an organization, it is natural to ask who is responsible. Unfortunately, some organizations are designed to produce scapegoats—forced ranking systems, for instance, create all kinds of competition between employees, and not all of it is helpful or friendly. And treating behavior as if it exclusively means worker behavior creates blind spots. Incident investigations contribute to the problem when they stop as soon as a worker's behavior is identified as a "root cause." In many cases, like the one we are describing, behavior is not even close to the root cause. Failure to see the real root cause leads to short-sighted solutions that often make the situation worse. If this had happened in the metal recycling plant, the maintenance worker would have been disciplined for his blatant disregard of procedures. The maintenance team may have received training on the proper procedure, and management may have told employees (again) that they should not proceed with work that they believe to be unsafe. However, these "solutions" would have done nothing to provide a safer workplace because the worker's action was only the end of the story, while the prevention opportunity was back at the beginning.

What really happened was this: Blades striking the sidewalls were known to be an issue for years. Blades were wearing out with increasing frequency, and each time workers replaced them they'd find more evidence that they had been scraping the inside of the blender. Workers had put out several small fires inside the blender, fires that were caused by sparks from the blades scraping the sidewall. This was a well-known issue and workers were not acting alone: Managers and supervisors had been consulted and a number of solutions had been tried. Management made the decision to continue without having found a solution, knowing it was leaving an unsafe workplace intact. At least once, when the maintenance department didn't have new blades in inventory, a decision was made to adjust the old blades so that they wouldn't strike the sidewalls. Nobody expected the adjustment to hold, but they made a decision to put the machine back into operation anyway. When they did eventually replace the parts, they found a large crack in the side wall of the machine, presumably caused by the stress of the blades striking it. A decision was made to weld the crack and return the machine to operation. On the day of the explosion, the maintenance worker was doing exactly what he had learned to do over all these years: Keep the blender going, use old parts if necessary, feel free to improvise (i.e. deviate from procedures). Nobody would question him, in fact he would be regarded as a hero, if he could defer replacement and maximize uptime. And this is just the blender issue: There were several other known issues—dust management in the plant, materials storage, emergency response, enforcement of rules—each with its own history, each on its own making the plant a dangerous place to work.

A shallow focus on behavior brings attention to the endpoint, but it does not tell you how to improve it. If you want to improve behavior, you need to change what is driving it, and to understand that, we need to be able to see the decisions that cause it. At that point, management has to have the courage to face the issue and take on the real safety task of creating a safe workplace.

USING BEHAVIOR-BASED SAFETY EFFECTIVELY: ORGANIZATIONAL BEHAVIOR RATHER THAN WORKER BEHAVIOR

When done correctly, behavior-based safety captures information about the drivers of behavior—information about the facility, organizational systems, culture, and leadership. This information is frequently and systematically analyzed, action plans are developed, and tangible improvements to the facility, equipment, tools, systems, culture, and leadership are implemented. These data-driven, practical changes to improve people's ability to do their work make the workplace safer. And in our experience, the more of this kind of effort in a behavior-based safety process, the better the results.

None of this is to deny the importance of the safe behavior the worker in and of itself. Given the best design possible—the best safety systems, culture, and leadership—the worker still has to perform safely. Standing out of harm's way is essential. Seat belts must be worn in cars. Handrails must be used when descending staircases. Understanding the role of safe behavior doesn't mean ignoring unsafe behavior when the worker is fully given the opportunity to do the job safely. *Behavioral reliability,* the organization's ability to assure consistent behavior up, down, and across the organization, is crucially important.

But when we talk about behavior, the thing we should be most interested in is *organizational behavior.* In the case of the metal recycling plant, any other person in that facility would have done the same thing as the maintenance worker right before the dust explosion—which means it was not an individual issue, it was an organizational issue. This should come as good news to a senior leader who is looking for leverage to make improvements in safety. Behavior tells you if you have successfully made a safer workplace. If you do the right things, if you pull the right lever, you will see reliably safe behavior and better performance throughout your organization. So what is this lever?

THE STRONGEST LEVER IS LEADERSHIP

Nobody is in a better position to influence organizational performance than senior management. Senior leader decisions drive culture and systems, which in turn drive organizational behavior and performance.

It is a dynamic system. Change one part of the system, it will affect all of the other parts. For example, at the metal recycling plant, the senior leadership team could decide to start looking at maintenance logs and to free up money to address safety issues. Doing this would change basic assumptions about what is expected of workers and supervisors, about the importance of safety, and about how to handle work disruptions. Alternatively, the site manager could stop looking the other way when people deviate from procedures. Doing this would surface all kinds of discussion, and resolution, of the myriad of issues making it impossible for workers to follow procedures. This, in turn, would change assumptions and beliefs about how people should work and what is expected of them. The VP of operations could encourage building redundant equipment into the work process—purchasing extra machines, stocking replacement parts, having contingency plans—so that equipment could be taken out of service when issues needed to be addressed. This would directly affect how people work, and the culture surrounding that. Or, the CEO could resolve to change her culture from a "make do" culture to a "make right" culture. If she did this well, the other facility, systems, and leadership issues would surface and get resolved. For any of this to happen, people in the organization need to recognize the problem was not the installation of a bad blade in the blending machine: The problem was rooted in a dynamic system comprised of the physical environment, leadership, culture, systems, and behavior.

The insight here is that it is worth it for senior leaders to understand behavior: they need to know what it is, and why it is important. Understanding that should cause leaders to teach their organizations to dig much deeper into systems, culture, and indeed their own leadership.

When organizational behavior is examined closely across levels, something very interesting emerges: As you go up in responsibility, the essence of action shifts from overt observable behavior towards decision making. For the front-line employee, safe behavior speaks for itself; the worker wears protective equipment or doesn't, follows the procedure or doesn't. Even with the first-line supervisor, safe action starts to shift to decisions. Does the supervisor approve a permit? This action is more a decision than a behavior. Are resources allocated by the plant manager for safety related maintenance? Is safety strategy given a major place in the overall strategy of the company? Do board meetings have safety on their agenda? All these things are driven by senior leader decisions.

Humans have built-in tendencies to over- and under-estimate the importance of different factors that influence critical decisions. The result is that safe decision-making is compromised. In the next chapter we discuss safe decision making and how cognitive biases operate to undermine it.

REFERENCES

i Krause, T.R., Hidley, J. H. & Hodson, S. J. (1990). *The behavior-based safety process: Managing involvement for an injury-free culture*, 1st ed. New York: Van Nostrand Reinhold.

CHAPTER 7

SAFE DECISION MAKING AND COGNITIVE BIAS

In the last chapter we explored the complexity of achieving safe behavior in the workplace. We outlined principles that define the role of behavior in organizational safety. Here we will consider a more fundamental aspect of the human performance equation: safe decision making. While behavior tends to be misunderstood as only "front-line employee behavior," decision making is easier to see running up, down, and across the organization. Safe decisions are critically important at all levels, and the higher up, the more influential the decision. It isn't good if I decide not to wear a seat belt in the car I'm driving, but it is a disaster if I decide not to equip the company fleet with seat belts.

Recent research in the behavioral and social sciences, including neuroscience, has shown us that the basic processes that guide human decision making are in themselves flawed. These flaws, which researchers call "cognitive biases" are not mistakes or errors, they are chronic ways of thinking that produce inaccurate judgments, and they apply directly to safety judgments and decisions.

The 7th insight is that *safe decision making plays a critical role in performance and is undermined by cognitive bias*. Human brains naturally use shortcuts that allow us to take in massive amounts of information and process it all quickly and efficiently. That's generally useful, but these same shortcuts trade off speed for accuracy, and they lead to predictable biases in judgment. This process of flawed judgments is constantly at work in judgments about uncertainty and risk. In this chapter, we explore the role of cognitive biases and how they affect judgments and decisions about safety.

ESTIMATING RISK

A great many safety-related decisions start with probability estimates. The research in cognitive bias shows that probability estimates are extremely sensitive to bias. "Risk" is in itself a statement of probability. When I assess a risk, I make a judgment about a probability.

For example, is it a good idea for my son or daughter to start driving a car at age 16? How do I go about making this important safety-related decision? The concern that I have is about her age. I want her to learn to drive. But is she ready to start now? Probably I make that decision based on my assessment of the maturity level of my daughter. Is she emotionally stable, does she have the ability to pay attention, is she overly influenced by her peers? If I come to the conclusion that she is mature enough, I tend to think driving is okay.

These are important considerations, but they probably aren't the most central ones. In fact, thinking about it this way is to fall victim to cognitive bias. The question I don't ask myself is this one: How frequently do 16 year olds have serious or fatal accidents, in contrast to drivers that are say 17, 18, or 25? In other words, before I consider special circumstances or mitigating factors, what is the baseline rate of accident frequency for this age group? That is the rate that I should consider when making this decision (Figure 9).

With an aging parent, the issue we are getting at is easier to see. When my father gets to be 75 I start to worry, not about his maturity but about the fact that 75 year olds are often not terrific drivers. I am concerned with his declining perceptual and motor skills and the declining safety performance of his cohort, not his personality.

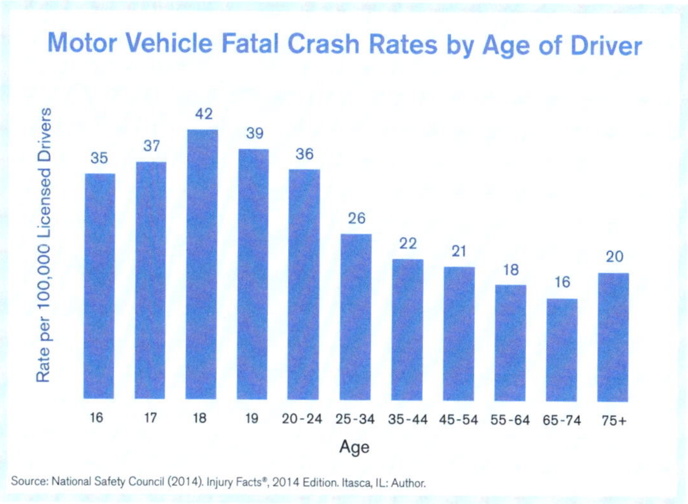

Figure 9

Our point isn't to tell you what to decide. The point we are making is that it is natural and normal, though biased, to overlook the most relevant data when making this safety decision. The bias is called *Failure to Consider the Baseline*, and it has been well researched over the last 30 years. The mental short cut that we are all inclined to take is to overlook critical baseline data for the thing we are considering.

Now that you understand this principle, consider the following from Daniel Kahneman's *Thinking, Fast and Slow*. An individual has been described by a neighbor as follows: "Steve is very shy and withdrawn, invariably helpful but with little interest in people or in the world of reality. A meek and tidy soul, he has a need for order and structure, and a passion for detail." Is it more likely that Steve is a farmer or a librarian?

Having just read about cognitive bias, some readers will answer this question correctly. The ratio of male farmers to male librarians in the US is 20:1, so chances are Steve is a farmer. Interestingly, others will nonetheless answer incorrectly. Cognitive bias is a challenge to overcome, and it is a critical challenge to those who want to see safety performance improvement.

OVERCONFIDENCE BIAS AND UNDERESTIMATING RISK

How good a driver are you? Compared to other drivers on the road, are you above average or below average? If you said "above average," you and 93% of American drivers believe you are above average.[i] Humans are hard-wired to overestimate their own skills and abilities. We see a vapor coming out of the vent, but decide the leak isn't sufficiently large to warrant immediate action. We're short-staffed, so instead of running two continuous mining machines side by side, we decide to use one mining machine and keep repositioning it without giving the workers additional support. Maintaining positive views of ourselves helps us cope with adversity and helps us thrive, but unfortunately it also causes us to make poor judgments about risk. This is what cognitive psychologists call *Overconfidence Bias.*

Overconfidence Bias shows up in safety in a wide variety of ways. For instance, the plant manager who makes cuts in the maintenance budget thinking it won't matter. The division leader who thinks an incentive program will solve safety issues. Or the CEO who thinks that safety is doing well because recordable injury frequencies are declining. It also shows up in more subtle ways. One way to detect it is by listening to your own thoughts and to what people around you say. A few signs of Overconfidence Bias you might hear are:

> "I understand safety as well as our safety people do."
>
> "Our safety systems are first rate."
>
> "We haven't had a fatality in three years."

"This training doesn't apply to me."

"We've done it like this for 30 years, and I haven't been injured."

"We're having stupid injuries. But if we just get the behavior right, they will go away."

"That would never happen here."

The first step to overcoming Overconfidence Bias is to teach people about it. That will open the door to building a culture in which it is okay to challenge it. You want people to have enough understanding of bias to recognize it and incorporate it into how they talk about risk.

DEFAULTS AND RECOGNIZING CHANGES IN EXPOSURE TO RISK

Another way that bias affects safe decision making is the dramatic role of the *default*. A default is a pre-selected option. We frequently see defaults in computer software, for instance. When installing the software, we are given the choice to use the "default setup" provided by the software manufacturers. If you've ever set up a computer, you know that default options are faster and easier than going through a custom setup.

Research on how defaults affect decision making is telling: People tend to choose the default option, no matter what it is. In effect, the leader who controls the default has an opportunity to control the decision of the user by the way that alternatives are presented. For example, this is why when you fill out a form on a website, there is often a box already checked that says, "Yes, please send me marketing material." You have to look for the box and un-select it if you want to keep your inbox clean. The

US government requires marketers to get permission to use our email for marketing purposes, but marketers know that they will get permission from the most people if they present us the option already selected.

A more subtle form of a default used to control decision making is to present people with a couple of options, both of which imply acceptance of a third option. Parents are famous for this: "Johnny, would you like your broccoli with cheese or with bacon?" Johnny has to go out of his way to "opt out" of having any broccoli at all.

Safety leaders can use defaults to influence safe decisions. Many do already, instinctively. You probably offer your employees a choice of the type of safety glasses, but not the choice to have them. It is expected that everyone will participate in a training program, even though they could actually opt out. The safety guard on a machine is locked and the machine is turned off until the operator holds a button on the grip, but the guard reverts to locked and off if the hand comes off. That's a good thing. Those defaults are useful. But poorly designed defaults can work to the disadvantage of safety.

Do your employees ever re-use pre-task risk assessments? If so, the previous risk assessment is acting as a default and probably getting in the way of people seeing the exposure with fresh eyes. If a supervisor receives a work permit already filled out, she is more likely to sign it without walking through the site. If it's not already on her schedule, she is less likely to find time for things that come up.

In order to deal with defaults, your organization needs to closely examine where they are throughout your procedures, instructions, training materials, permit systems, and all other communications related to safety. Then you need to re-design these communications to influence safety appropriately.

AVAILABILITY BIAS AND INVESTING TIME AND MONEY IN SAFETY

Look at the safety communications throughout your organization. That means emails from senior leaders, posters, newsletters, and talks given at locations by visiting senior leaders. Are you—and your corporate leaders, site managers, supervisors, and safety leaders—giving people the best information about your most significant opportunities for safety improvement, your most significant exposures, and the risks you are most concerned about? If not, you may be biasing people's perception of risk through *Availability Bias.*

Availability Bias is the tendency to give too much weight to the information that is readily available. For example, a team at the University of Oregon found that people overestimated the likelihood of dying in a plane crash after major media coverage of those events.[ii] Another study showed that a firm's engineers misdiagnosed product failures because they tended to focus on recent experience, which was more readily available to them than earlier experience.[iii]

The Accident Cycle is a common example of how Availability Bias wreaks havoc with organizational attention to safety. Most of us have experienced an urgency to improve safety when injury rates are high. People respond to the urgency by shifting resources and attention, which are usually effective in bringing the injury rates down again, at least temporarily. As injury rates decline, the urgency fades, attention wanes, and issues resurface that bring injury rates back up until the cycle repeats. Unless we have systems in place to help maintain consistent focus and attention, the most recent experience is most readily available and tends to drive an organization's efforts in safety.

Here's another example: Do the senior leaders of your organization tend to emphasize things related to recent incidents that have occurred? In one company we worked with, a group of executives visiting a plant site walked around the employee parking lot with clipboards, checking for people taking risks. They thought of themselves as showing their interest and commitment to safety. Earlier that quarter there had been three minor injuries that involved employees walking in the parking lot. Availability Bias, remembering and focusing on the last thing that happened, was probably operating here. In this case it lowered leadership credibility, because employees knew of much more important safety concerns. They also knew that executive time is scarce and their ability to address safety issues is high. So the more effective intervention would have been to give executives direct experience with those operations dealing with the most challenging safety environments.

BIAS AND UNDERESTIMATING CUMULATIVE RISK

Leaders tend to view risk at the level of the individual worker and the individual situation. What is the probability of an injury occurring today when a group of maintenance mechanics change out a pump? This kind of thought comes up when the work configuration's design is called into question. Someone points out the problematic work setting and leaders then tend to think about the probability that an injury will occur in that work setting. But they often think about it as one work crew on one day. Yet, while the chance of an incident that day from that job is minute, the cumulative probability is greater than one would expect. This is largely because people are wired to underestimate *Cumulative Risk*. The better question is: If we continue to do maintenance jobs allowing this kind of work environment, what is the probability of an incident?

Think about the tragic outcomes from Deepwater Horizon. Leaders and supervisors made a series of poor safety decisions trying to keep it on schedule. Experience taught them that the compromises they were making were very unlikely to be detected, and even less likely to cause a catastrophic blowout. But the cumulative risk of those compromises, taken industry-wide, made the disaster entirely predictable.

CONFIRMATION BIAS AND PRE-TASK RISK ASSESSMENTS

Several years ago, a miner with over 30 years' experience died when the roof of a tunnel he was working in gave way. Before starting the work, he and a foreman inspected the tunnel's roof structure for issues and found none. After the incident, the risk assessment was repeated, but this time, 137 missing bolts and compromised roof planks were identified. Had they seen the risk, but convinced themselves nothing bad would happen to them that day? Or had they just not expected to find any problems during their pre-task risk assessment? To the extent they had not seen the hazard because they didn't expect to, *Confirmation Bias* was the culprit.

We have read hundreds of investigation reports related to serious injuries and fatalities. Weak pre-task risk assessments show up over and over again in these reports. People tend to look for what they know (Availability Bias) and find what they expect (Confirmation Bias). The International Labour Organization estimates that over two million workers die each year around the world, which means even a small improvement in this single issue could save tens of thousands of lives.[iv]

The insight here is that safety-related decisions are easily undermined by cognitive biases that are built into each and every one of us. This chapter examined several cognitive biases and the ways that they affect risk perception and decision making.

Throughout this book, we have advocated for gathering data, analyzing it, and doing trend analyses in order to support informed, unbiased decisions. The availability of massive amounts of data from social media and the internet have sparked innovations in data warehousing, computer programming, and software development that take statistical analysis to a new dimension. In the final chapter, we discuss the opportunities and challenges with data analytics to make safer workplaces.

REFERENCES

i Svenson, O. (1981). Are we less risky and more skillful than our fellow drivers? *Acta Psychologica, 47*, 143-151.

ii Renn, O., Burns, W. J., Kasperson, J. X., Kasperson, R. E., & Slovic, P. (1992). The social amplification of risk: theoretical foundations and empirical applications. *Journal Of Social Issues, 48*(4), 137-160.

iii Roberto, M. 2002. Lessons from everest: the interaction of cognitive bias, psychological safety, and system complexity. *California Management Review*, 45(1), 136-158.

iv http://www.ilo.org/global/topics/safety-and-health-at-work/lang--en/index.htm

CHAPTER 8

CONCLUSION AND A LOOK FORWARD

Achieving organizational safety competence proceeds in predictable stages. Strong leadership improves safety systems, which leads to improvement in design and facilities. These things create a culture that brings out the best in people. Part of that culture is a value for innovation. Making major improvements almost always takes innovative ideas from talented leaders. Getting to zero fatal and serious injuries will take this kind of innovation. In this final chapter, we'll look ahead to the role emerging technologies will play in advancing workplace safety.

THE TECHNOLOGY OF THE LAST 10 YEARS PRESENTS NEW OPPORTUNITIES TO INNOVATE

Advances in data acquisition, storage, integration, and analysis; imaging technologies; sensors; and geospatial technologies have the potential to be adapted to serve safety goals. Decision science, and research from social psychology and neuroscience, set the stage for innovations with new methodologies and new ideas. What's more, there are longstanding concepts from socio-technical theory have never been fully integrated into organizational safety, yet show great potential. New research that demonstrates which are the most potent components of BBS (rightly constructed) offers particular potential for advances in safety outcomes. Combinations of these methods can and will be powerful.

Some of these new technologies are already saving lives. Hospitals are making real progress using new technology and analytics to monitor and increase hand-washing by physicians and other caregivers. Researchers estimate that if the technology were implemented across US hospitals, more than 70,000 lives could be saved every year.[i]

Furthermore, police departments are using analytics to anticipate when and where crime will take place, enabling preventative action.[ii] Cities are using big data to measure pollution and then making the data available to the public so that, for example, they can factor it into choices about where to live.[iii]

Throughout this book, we have advocated using data to support informed, unbiased decisions. Traditional methods for collecting data about organizational behavior (including observations, inspections, web-based surveys, interviews, and focus groups) are time-consuming. New technology allows data to be collected much more consistently and easily, but as yet it is underutilized for safety. There are opportunities to make better use of data science well within our reach.

Imagine never having to fill out another 360 leadership survey. Instead, you walk down the hall and have a conversation with someone, walk back to your office and look at your smartphone. On your screen is a safety leadership score based on your words, your body language, and the other person's response to you. You see a score on how influential you were, followed by practices you can use to increase your influence. The technology for this exists: In 2009, a group of researchers from MIT demonstrated how wearable sensors could capture individual and group behavior. In a study of 67 nurses, data from the wearable sensors correlated with personality characteristics, workload, productivity, stress, teamwork, and even patient outcomes.[iv]

Imagine never having to fill out another behavioral observation datasheet. What if you had real-time information that would tell you what changes were needed to make improvements in workplace safety? Group-level problem solving is among the most important, yet underutilized, components of behavior-based improvement processes today. Technology exists to identify improvement opportunities, making data collection cheaper and problem solving stronger. With the help of cameras and sensors, data can be automatically collected, sorted, and channeled to problem-solving teams—with issues already identified and prioritized. Employees are directly engaged in the process of solving safety problems. The technology to do this is already being used in:

- Health and fitness
  (fitbit.com; jawbone.com; sleepcycle.com)

- Cars and trucks
  (driversafetycameras.com)

- Locomotives
  (metrolinktrains.com/pdfs/MetrolinkMatters/
  MetrolinkMattersFeb10.pdf)

- Hospitals
  (proventix.com)

- Management
  (sociometricsolutions.com/research1.html)

Advances like these in electronic monitoring open up a vast array of data. Advances in computer technology and software make it possible to process massive amounts of data quickly and efficiently. With these opportunities come new challenges: Who has the skills to program, capture, clean, store, and analyze these data? How will trust be earned and preserved amidst detailed data collection? These challenges require organizational culture, processes, staffing, and leadership to keep pace with changes in technology.

A NEW SAFETY PROFESSION: THE SAFETY DATA SCIENTIST

Big data brings new opportunities for safety professionals, whose role is both important and constantly changing. No longer is it sufficient for us to enforce safety regulations and standards; safety professionals must be able to influence with and without authority, and to advise and collaborate with operational managers in their efforts to reduce and manage exposure.

Safety departments must change as well. The data that they collect and generate must inform more sophisticated questions. No longer is it enough to maintain OSHA logs, enter data into a computerized incident tracking system, and tally numbers on scorecards for management. Safety departments need safety data scientists: They need people who have the skills to program devices, capture usable data, and turn it into predictive models. Safety professionals will need to understand the scientific method so that they can use the data to test hypotheses and help deliver insights to the organization's managers and executives.

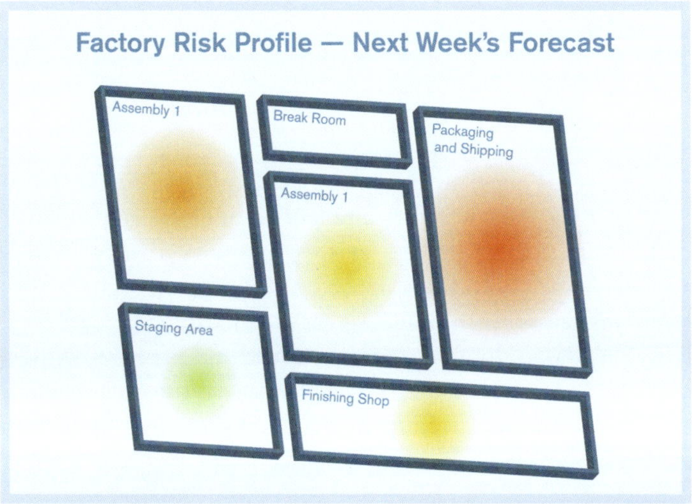

Figure 10

Imagine instead of receiving reports about past incidents, receiving forecasts of workplace safety. Like weather forecasts, exposure forecasts could integrate information about upcoming work, staff experience, risk profiles, the robustness of safety management systems, culture, and even local leadership. Such a map could be used to allocate safety resources, plan safety activities, or optimize schedules for the upcoming week (Figure 10).

A NEW KIND OF INCIDENT INVESTIGATION

Our ability to learn after things go wrong will always be a crucial part of safety management. Yet incident investigation methods have not kept up with improving knowledge about incident causation, let alone emerging technologies. Incident investigations at present are heavily dependent on who is investigating and why, and they vary greatly in what they look for and what they find.

Naturally, investigators look for the things that they know most about. For example, review the publicly available fatality investigations on the Mine Safety and Health Administration website, and you will find a strong focus on compliance with MSHA standards. MSHA's investigations, like most, tend to stop at the immediate root causes, and fail to ask why those root causes were tolerated in the first place. Historically, investigations discover very little about culture or leadership practices and their impact on the incident. Perhaps most problematic of all, reports are heavily biased towards "findings." Rarely do they report on "non-findings" which are equally important if one is going to aggregate reports and use the data to test hypotheses. Technology can change all of this. Organizations can start by adopting standardized incident investigation tools that go beyond the first layer of causes and compliance with standards. Organizations can work together to identify and systematically capture contextual data that can be aggregated and used later on.

NEW SAFETY LEADERSHIP PRACTICES

The proliferation of data gathering devices in work environments raises questions about privacy, transparency, and worker motivation. Whereas sensors in public places can feel anonymous even when they are not, sensors at work can feel personal even when they are anonymous. Leaders will need to hone new leadership practices in order to make people feel safe, secure, and motivated in a sensor-rich environment. Anonymity may not be enough; granting employees access to the data may prove important in getting full value from it, while also fostering trust and engagement from employees.

Used well, the data may be just as powerful for individuals as it is for organizations. Workers will have new tools for increasing self-awareness and individual influence. As our experience with big data grows, more safety leadership practices will emerge regarding how leaders gather, share, collaborate with, and communicate data. All of this can be incredibly empowering or it can be threatening. Leaders should not shy away from these opportunities, nor should they skirt these issues.

Technology continues to change the world of safety, particularly when it comes to how we gather and use data. What it doesn't change is our value for people, our commitment to safety, or our duties to respect and protect human dignity and privacy. Organizations must seize the opportunities to use data to improve safety and in particular prevent injuries, illnesses, and fatalities. Their leaders must ensure technology is implemented in ways that preserve the values they are charged to uphold.

Studying incidents, from minor injuries to very serious and fatal events, has taught us that it is possible to make major leaps forward in organizational safety competence. There is nothing inevitable about the incidents you see in organizations today.

The question is whether or not leadership has the information required to foster and sustain a culture of safety, the vision to see that innovation is necessary, and the insights essential to making it reality.

REFERENCES

i Dai, H., Milkman, K. L., Hofmann, D. A., & Staats, B. R. (2015). The impact of time at work and time off from work on rule compliance: The case of hand hygiene in health care. *Journal Of Applied Psychology*, 100(3), 846-862. doi:10.1037/a0038067

ii Hollywood, J. S., Smith, S. C., Price, C., McInnis, B., Perry, W. (2012). Predictive policing: What it is, what it isn't, and where it can be useful [PowerPoint Presentation]. Retrieved from http://www.theiacp.org/Portals/0/pdfs/LEIM/2012Presentations/OPS-PredictivePolicing.pdf

iii Dwoskin, E. (2014, October 21). They're tracking when you turn off the lights. *Wall Street Journal* (Online). p. 1. Retrieved from http://online.wsj.com/articles/theyre-tracking-when-you-turn-off-the-lights-1413854422

iv Olguin, D., Gloor, P. A., & Pentland, A. S. (2009, March). Capturing individual and group behavior with wearable sensors. *AAAI Spring Symposium on Human Behavior Modeling*. Retrieved from http://www.aaai.org/Papers/Symposia/Spring/2009/SS-09-04/SS09-04-012.pdf

INDEX

Symbols

A

B

C

D

E

F

G

H

I

J

K

L

M

N

O

P

Q

R

S

T

U

V

W

Z